A Book of
Luminous Things

OTHER BOOKS BY CZESLAW MILOSZ

The Captive Mind

Selected Poems

Native Realm

The Issa Valley

Emperor of the Earth

Visions from San Francisco Bay

Bells in Winter

Separate Notebooks

The Unattainable Earth

Collected Poems

The Land of Ulro

Provinces

The Witness of Poetry

Beginning with My Streets

A Year of the Hunter

Facing the River

A Book of Luminous Things

AN INTERNATIONAL ANTHOLOGY
OF POETRY

Edited and with an introduction by

Czeslaw Milosz

A HARVEST BOOK

HARCOURT, INC.

Orlando Austin New York San Diego London

For information about permission to reproduce selections from this book,
write to trade.permissions@hmhco.com or to Permissions,
Houghton Mifflin Harcourt Publishing Company,
3 Park Avenue, 19th Floor, New York, New York 10016.

Permissions acknowledgments appear on pp. 307–314.

www.hmhco.com

Library of Congress Cataloging-in-Publication Data
A Book of luminous things: an international anthology of poetry/edited
and with an introduction by Czeslaw Milosz.
p.   cm.
Includes index.
ISBN 978-0-15-100169-9
ISBN 978-0-15-600574-6 (pbk.)
1. Poetry—Collections.   I. Milosz, Czeslaw.
PN6101.B585   1996   95-38060
808.81—dc20

Text set in Spectrum
Designed by Lori McThomas Buley

Printed in the United States of America
First Harvest edition 1998
DOC 30 29
4500701184

ACKNOWLEDGMENTS

I wish to express my gratitude to persons who helped me in compiling this anthology. My friend and co-translator of my poetry, Robert Hass, encouraged me and worked with me on the English versions of some poems. At his suggestion, we jointly taught a graduate seminar in the English Department of the University of California at Berkeley in 1993 using the poems of this anthology as material for our sessions. The enthusiastic reactions of students gave me a new assurance as to the value of my judgments. Another Berkeley poet and friend, Leonard Nathan, closely followed my endeavors and drew my attention to several poems fitting my purpose.

Work on the anthology, from its beginning, received warm support from my wife, Carol, who also offered advice, helped type the early manuscript draft, and organized the many details necessary to complete this project. Kimball Fenn, a graduate student in the English Department at Berkeley, brought her intelligent assistance, competence, and diligence to typing, editing, and compiling the permissions' citations for the manuscript.

CONTENTS

INTRODUCTION

I have always felt that a poet participates in the management of the estate of poetry, of that in his own language and also that of world poetry. Thinking about that estate, such as it is at the present moment, I decided I could contribute to its possessions provided, however, that instead of theory, I brought to it something of practice.

Poetry in this century is alive, and I value many poets, some of whom I have translated into Polish, beginning with T. S. Eliot's *Waste Land* and *Burnt Norton*. Yet no poem by T. S. Eliot is included in this book, and this fact elucidates my purpose. I rejected in advance the idea of doing justice to the canon of today's American and World poetry. Many poems that I like or admire are not in this anthology because they do not correspond to my criteria of size and accessibility to the reader. I leave to others the exploration of the whole territory of poetry in its richness and variety. I, instead, carve from it a province of my own.

For many decades I have been an observer of and a participant in revolts, movements, schools, whatever their names, in the literature of the twentieth century. Here, I try to forget about those trends. My proposition consists in presenting poems, whether contemporary or a thousand years old, that are, with few exceptions, short, clear, readable and, to use a compromised term, realist, that is, loyal toward reality and attempting to describe it as concisely as possible. Thus they undermine the widely held opinion that poetry is a misty domain eluding understanding. I act like an art collector who, to spite the devotees of abstract art, arranges an exhibition of figurative painting, putting together canvases from various epochs to prove, since those from the past and from the present meet in an unexpected way, that certain lines of development, different from those now universally accepted, can be traced.

My intention is not so much to defend poetry in general, but, rather, to remind readers that for some very good reasons it may be of importance today. These reasons have to do with our troubles in the present phase of our civilization.

It has happened that we have been afflicted with a basic *deprivation*, to such an extent that we seem to be missing some vital organs, even as we try to survive somehow. Theology, science, philosophy, though they attempt to provide cures, are not very effective "In that dark world where gods have lost their way" (Roethke). They are able at best to confirm that our affliction is not invented. I have written elsewhere of this deprivation as one of the consequences brought about by science and technology that pollutes not only the natural environment but also the human imagination. The world deprived of clear-cut outlines, of the up and the down, of good and evil, succumbs to a peculiar nihilization, that is, it loses its colors, so that grayness covers not only things of this earth and of space, but also the very flow of time, its minutes, days, and years. Abstract considerations will be of little help, even if they are intended to bring relief. Poetry is quite different. By its very nature it says: All those theories are untrue. Since poetry deals with the singular, not the general, it cannot— if it is good poetry—look at things of this earth other than as colorful, variegated, and exciting, and so, it cannot reduce life, with all its pain, horror, suffering, and ecstasy, to a unified tonality of boredom or complaint. By necessity poetry is therefore on the side of being and against nothingness.

The place where I gathered my hoard is not without significance. To some degree it explains the contents. Berkeley has, probably, the best bookstores in America, and also good libraries, including the libraries of theological schools of various denominations. Its university constantly reminds one that California faces the Pacific, something to which the number of students from Chinese, Japanese, or Vietnamese families testifies. To this should be added the role of Buddhism in the somewhat too syncretic mosaic of religions. Besides, Berkeley possesses a quite high density of poets per square mile. As a consequence of all this, its bookstores afford a good opportunity to browse in poetry. I have found there also many translations of Asian poets, who have sympathetic readers here. Those volumes distinguish themselves favorably upon the background of poetry written in our epoch. Old Chinese and Japanese poetry has exerted an influence upon American poetry since the beginning of this century, and became a field of competition for ambitious translators, among whom the best known are an Englishman, Sir Arthur Waley, and the California poet Kenneth Rexroth.

What do we, shaped by a civilization so different, find in those masters, what attracts us to them in particular? Undoubtedly, what accounts for much is the very discovery that we can understand them, that through their lips eternal man speaks, that love, transience, death were the same then as now. Yet what is also valuable for us in them is the reminder that man may relate to the world not just through confrontation. Perhaps Taoism and Buddhism, with their contemplative leanings, enabled poets to look at a thing and identify with it, strengthening in that way its being. The very reminder of it directs our attention toward similar attitudes within our civilization—and they are not rare, either in poetry or in painting.

Paul Cézanne is considered a forerunner of twentieth-century painting. It is probable, though, that he, since he was inclined to outbursts of anger, would horribly abuse his successors for their betrayal of nature, his venerated mistress. He invoked Boileau and recited: *Rien n'est beau que le vrai, le vrai seul est aimable* (Beauty is only in the true, only the true is lovable). "My method, my code," he declared, "is realism." And against disintegration of the object into fragments in consequence of the discoveries of science, he would probably allow me to quote his opinion: "After all, am I not man? Whatever I do, I have the notion that this tree is a tree, this rock a rock, this dog a dog." Or: "Nature is not on the surface, it is inside. Colors, on the surface, show that inside. They show the roots of the world." And again this: "Right now a moment of time is fleeting by. Capture its reality in paint! To do that we must put all else out of our minds. We must become that moment, make ourselves a sensitive recording plate . . . give the image of what we actually see, forgetting everything that has been before our time" (in Joachim Gasquet, *Cézanne*). If readers find in my book poems fulfilling Cézanne's advice, I will be pleased. What surprises me in his pronouncement is the stress laid on the moment—by a painter. Time thus appears to be composed of moments—things, or things-moments. And the artist in his work has to capture and to preserve one moment, which becomes, indeed, eternal. In that way time is valorized; its every small part deserves an alert noting down of its shape and color.

In my essays on the beginning of the nineteenth century I stand for "classicism" against "romanticism." And this authorizes me to quote the praise of objective art pronounced then by Goethe in his conversations with Ackerman: "We are bid to study the ancients; yet what does that avail us, if it does not teach us to study the real world, and reproduce that?—for there was the source of the power of the ancients." "I will now tell you something, of which I think you will find frequent confirmation in your experience. When eras are on the decline, all tendencies are subjective; but, on the other hand, when matters are ripening for a new epoch, all tendencies are objective. Our present time is retrograde, therefore subjective; we see this now more clearly in poetry than in painting, and other ways. Each manly effort, on the contrary, turns its force from the inward to the outward world. In important eras, those who have striven and acted most manfully were all objective in their nature" (translated by Margaret Fuller, 1852). It is difficult to dismiss lightly that affirmation, especially if one thinks—as I do—that the end of the "objective" order in music occurred precisely at the time of Goethe.

Another name I may invoke is Schopenhauer. How could I not acknowledge his influence if I looked to him (in this I was not alone) for praise of art as a remedy against the cruelty of life? We are today skeptical of "systems," but his vision of the universe as

Will was born in the mind of a man particularly sensitive to pain and suffering as the universal law. The famous pessimism of Schopenhauer comes from a compassionate observation of live beings crushed and crushing each other because of the Will seated in them; in other words, "the instinct of self-preservation," "the struggle for life," and so on. Schopenhauer is our contemporary, for he was the first to draw conclusions from the biological sciences (a Darwinist before Darwin). At the same time he was the first European philosopher open to the religions of India, and his theory of art is somewhat similar to the saving message of Prince Siddhartha called Buddha, who offered to humans liberation from suffering by stepping beyond the infernal circle of fears and desires. Artists, according to Schopenhauer, are committed to a completely "unpractical" activity. In order to attain beauty they rid themselves for a moment of those urges to which as human beings they are all subject. Art liberates and purifies, and its tokens are those short moments when we look at a beautiful landscape forgetting about ourselves, when everything that concerns us disappears, is dissolved, and it does not matter whether the eye that looks is that of a beggar or a king.

Among works of painting, Schopenhauer assigned the highest place to Dutch *still life*: "Inward disposition, the predominance of knowing over willing, can produce this state under any circumstances. This is shown by those admirable Dutch artists who directed this purely objective perception to the most insignificant objects, and established a lasting monument of their objectivity and spiritual peace in their pictures of *still life*, which the aesthetic beholder does not look on without emotion; for they present to him the peaceful, still frame of mind of the artists, free from will, which was needed to contemplate such insignificant things so objectively, to observe them so attentively, and to repeat this perception so intelligently."

The secret of all art, also of poetry, is, thus, distance. Thanks to distance the past preserved in our memory is purified and embellished. When what we remember was occurring, reality was considerably less enticing, for we were tossed, as usual, by anxieties, desires, and apprehensions that colored everything, people, institutions, landscapes. Remembering, we move to that land of past time, yet now without our former passions: we do not strive for anything, we are not afraid of anything, we become an eye which perceives and finds details that had escaped our attention.

I do not pretend, though, that in selecting poems for this book I constantly kept in mind Schopenhauer's principles, because many texts included depart from those principles.

The word "objective" repeated in the quotations from both Goethe and Schopenhauer is, I suspect, used for lack of a better term, though we understand, more or less, what those authors wanted to say. In the nineteen-twenties a group of "objectivists" was active in New York, with a program advocating attention to objects that surround us (note the famous "Red Wheelbarrow" of William Carlos Williams), but this proves only how various can be the uses of the word "object." Though some poems of "objectivists" are included in my selection, I do not have any intention of subsuming the whole under any all-embracing category, of objective, antisubjective poetry, or something of the kind. Yet, since I am obviously interested in the visible world, again and again unveiling itself and offering itself to the eye, I would have nothing against calling my anthology a book of enchantments.

Epiphany

Epiphany is an unveiling of reality. What in Greek was called *epiphaneia* meant the appearance, the arrival, of a divinity among mortals or its recognition under a familiar shape of man or woman. Epiphany thus interrupts the everyday flow of time and enters as one privileged moment when we intuitively grasp a deeper, more essential reality hidden in things or persons. A poem-epiphany tells about one moment-event and this imposes a certain form.

A polytheistic antiquity saw epiphanies at every step, for streams and woods were inhabited by dryads and nymphs, while the commanding gods looked and behaved like humans, were endowed with speech, could, though with difficulty, be distinguished from mortals, and often walked the earth. Not rarely, they would visit households and were recognized by hosts. The Book of Genesis tells about a visit paid by God to Abraham, in the guise of three travellers. Later on, the epiphany as appearance, the arrival of Christ, occupies an important place in the New Testament.

D. H. LAWRENCE
1885—1930

D. H. Lawrence in his "Maximus" returns to the polytheistic world, and the poem is so effective that we feel a shock of recognition, as if we ourselves were visited by the god Hermes. Maximus is the name of a philosopher who was a teacher of the emperor Julian, called the Apostate because he tried to restore paganism.

Epiphany may also mean a privileged moment in our life among the things of this world, in which they suddenly reveal something we have not noticed until now; and that something is like an intimation of their mysterious, hidden side. In a way, poetry is an attempt to break through the density of reality into a zone where the simplest things are again as fresh as if they were being seen by a child.

This anthology is full of epiphanies. I decided to place some of them in a separate first chapter to highlight this aspect of poetry. These particular poems are a distillation of my major theme.

MAXIMUS

God is older than the sun and moon
and the eye cannot behold him
nor voice describe him.

But a naked man, a stranger, leaned on the gate
with his cloak over his arm, waiting to be asked in.
So I called him: Come in, if you will!—
He came in slowly, and sat down by the hearth.
I said to him: And what is your name?—
He looked at me without answer, but such a loveliness
entered me, I smiled to myself, saying: He is God!
So he said: *Hermes!*

God is older than the sun and moon
and the eye cannot behold him
nor the voice describe him:
and still, this is the God Hermes, sitting by my hearth.

KIKAKU
1661—1707

In Japanese haiku there are often flashes, or glimpses, and things appear like lightning, or as if in the light of a flare: epiphanies of a landscape.

Above the boat,
bellies
of wild geese.

Translated from the Japanese by Lucien Stryk and Takashi Ikemoto

ISSA
1763—1827

From the bough
floating down river,
insect song.

Translated from the Japanese by Lucien Stryk and Takashi Ikemoto

JEAN FOLLAIN
1903—1971

It seems nothing peculiar happens when somebody walks on a road and kicks an empty can. But here, in French poet Jean Follain, this movement, like an immobilized frame of a film, suddenly opens into the cold of the cosmos. Because it is winter, the road is frozen, the keys are iron, the shoe is pointed, and the can itself is cold, empty.

MUSIC OF SPHERES

He was walking a frozen road
in his pocket iron keys were jingling
and with his pointed shoe absent-mindedly
he kicked the cylinder
of an old can
which for a few seconds rolled its cold emptiness
wobbled for a while and stopped
under a sky studded with stars.

Translated from the French by Czeslaw Milosz and Robert Hass

CARLOS DRUMMOND DE ANDRADE
1902—1987

This poem is like a joke and we are inclined, first, to smile, yet a moment of thought suffices to restore a serious meaning to such an encounter. It is enough to live truly intensely our meeting with a thing to preserve it forever in our memory.

IN THE MIDDLE OF THE ROAD

In the middle of the road there was a stone
there was a stone in the middle of the road
there was a stone
in the middle of the road there was a stone.

Never should I forget this event
in the life of my fatigued retinas.
Never should I forget that in the middle of the road
there was a stone
there was a stone in the middle of the road
in the middle of the road there was a stone.

Translated from the Portuguese by Elizabeth Bishop

Nature

Our attitude towards nature is not the same as that of our ancestors. The Book of Genesis authorizes man "to have dominion over the fish of the sea, and over the fowl of the air, and over the cattle, and over the earth, and over every creeping thing that prospereth upon the earth." The line separating man from the rest of living creatures remained firm for centuries, and as late as the seventeenth century Descartes considered animals to be living machines. With the progress of life sciences this line has become blurred. Man now realizes that our species shares with animals their physiology and their basic drives. Nature, as we approach it, has grown much more enigmatic: our feeling of kinship engenders both empathy and guilt. At the same time, Nature stands before us as the great Other, deprived of any notion of good and evil, and therefore perfectly innocent, even if it is *Natura Devorans* and *Natura Devorata,* the devouring and the devoured. We are akin to it and yet we are alienated by our consciousness—our curse and our blessing. And precisely this ambiguity in our relationship, marked by the warmth of closeness and by the cold of detached observation, transpires in many poems.

DAVID WAGONER
1926—

Alexander Wilson (1766–1813), who appears in this poem by David Wagoner, left Scotland, where in his youth he acquired popularity as a folk poet, for political reasons, and moved to America, where he dedicated himself to observing nature, particularly birds. His American Ornithology, *with hand-colored woodcuts, appeared in 1808. He was a great ornithologist before Audubon. The first half of the nineteenth century was, in Europe, as well, a time of beautiful atlases of nature, hand-colored. The poem in fact deals with the impossibility of mutual understanding between man and nature. The hunter-artist believes that the woodpecker should be killed so that it may exist in books. This would not be well received by the bird, who could have answered that his only, indivdual life is taken from him so that paper may preserve a portrait not of himself, but of his species. The artist, as an observing mind, participates in the misfortune of the bird, though at the same time he is a hot-blooded being, bound to the woodpecker by some kind of fraternity.*

THE AUTHOR OF *AMERICAN ORNITHOLOGY* SKETCHES A BIRD, NOW EXTINCT

(Alexander Wilson, Wilmington, N.C. 1809)

When he walked through town, the wing-shot bird he'd hidden
Inside his coat began to cry like a baby,
High and plaintive and loud as the calls he'd heard
While hunting it in the woods, and goodwives stared
And scurried indoors to guard their own from harm.

And the innkeeper and the goodmen in the tavern
Asked him whether his child was sick, then laughed.
Slapped knees, and laughed as he unswaddled his prize,
His pride and burden: an ivory-billed woodpecker
As big as a crow, still wailing and squealing.

Upstairs, when he let it go in his workroom,
It fell silent at last. He told at dinner
How devoted masters of birds drawn from the life
Must gather their flocks around them with a rifle
And make them live forever inside books.

Later, he found his bedspread covered with plaster
And the bird clinging beside a hole in the wall
Clear through to already-splintered weatherboards
And the sky beyond. While he tied one of its legs
To a table leg, it started wailing again.

And went on wailing as if toward cypress groves
While the artist drew and tinted on fine vellum
Its red cockade, gray claws, and sepia eyes
From which a white edge flowed to the lame wing
Like light flying and ended there in blackness.

He drew and studied for days, eating and dreaming
Fitfully through the dancing and loud drumming
Of an ivory bill that refused pecans and beetles,
Chestnuts and sweet-sour fruit of magnolias,
Riddling his table, slashing his fingers, wailing.

He watched it die, he said, with great regret.

David Wagoner seems to be seized by a passion for drawing birds in his verse, and reading him I think of my friend, a Swiss painter, Robert Hainard, who chose as his profession wandering with a notebook in the Alps to sleuth birds and animals, or my high-school classmate Leopold Pac-Pomarnacki, hunter and sketch artist, at one time a prisoner of the Soviet gulags, a soldier of the Polish army in Italy, and finally a forester in Poland. In a way, a poem is in one respect superior to a drawing, because it may follow a sequence of movements. The Northwest of the United States is the territory of Wagoner's observations: the love display of certain waterfowl, particularly interesting in grebes and loons—the latter a permanent part of the misty lakes of the north.

LOONS MATING

Their necks and their dark heads lifted into a dawn
Blurred smooth by mist, the loons
Beside each other are swimming slowly
In charmed circles, their bodies stretched under water
Through ripples quivering and sweeping apart
The gray sky now held close by the lake's mercurial threshold
Whose face and underface they share
In wheeling and diving tandem, rising together
To swell their breasts like swans, to go breasting forward
With beaks turned down and in, near shore,
Out of sight behind a windbreak of birch and alder,
And now the haunted uprisen wailing call,
And again, and now the beautiful sane laughter.

JEAN FOLLAIN
1903—1971

In French poet Jean Follain a kinship of man and bird is shown in the reverse order. The shapes and colors of singing birds lead to a reflection on the strangeness of the body of his lover. Besides, in poetry and folk songs a girl often appears as a bird—a nightingale (Philomela in Ovid), a turtledove, even a sparrow.

A TAXIDERMIST

A taxidermist is sitting
before the russet breasts
green and purple wings
of his song-birds
dreaming about his lover
with a body so different
yet so close sometimes
to the body of the birds
that it seemed to him
very strange
in its curves and its volumes
in its colors and its finery
and its shades . . .

Translated from the French by Czeslaw Milosz and Robert Hass

LI-YOUNG LEE
1957—

Li-Young Lee is an immigrant from China but he writes in English. Yet perhaps in his work there is a strong current of Asian poetry.

IRISES

1.

In the night, in the wind, at the edge of the rain,
I find five irises, and call them lovely.
As if a woman, once, lay by them awhile,
then woke, rose, went, the memory of hair
lingers on their sweet tongues.

I'd like to tear these petals with my teeth.
I'd like to investigate these hairy selves,
their beauty and indifference. They hold
their breath all their lives
and open, open.

2.

We are not lovers, not brother and sister,
though we drift hand in hand through a hall
thrilling and burning as thought and desire
expire, and, over this dream of life,
this life of sleep, we waken dying—
violet becoming blue, growing
black, black—all that
an iris ever prays,
when it prays,
to be.

ROBERT CREELEY
1926 —

Man confronting nature fears his foreignness and is ashamed of his intrusion. He would like to return to the earthly paradise before Adam's sin. This seems to be a very American dream, and Robert Creeley's poem pays tribute to that tradition.

LIKE THEY SAY

Underneath the tree on some
soft grass I sat, I

watched two happy
woodpeckers be dis-

turbed by my presence. And
why not, I thought to

myself, why
not.

ADAM ZAGAJEWSKI
1945—

We're separated from nature as if by a glass wall—and this is the subject of this Polish poet. Poets have always been fascinated by the incomprehensible behavior of some creatures, for instance, the moth, which strives toward light and burns itself in the flame of a candle or kerosene lamp. Thence come comparisons: Love, as a fire which lures the lovers to their destruction. Yet moths, because they come from darkness into our circle of light, are, at the same time, messengers of that which is the most other. In this poem, people have their small security in a lighted house, but beyond the window, immeasurable spaces of the cosmos stretch, and the moths are like visitors from other galaxies.

MOTHS

Moths watched us through
the window. Seated at the table,
we were skewered by their lambent gazes,
harder than their shattering wings.

You'll always be outside,
past the pane. And we'll be here within,
more and more in. Moths watched us
through the window, in August.

Translated from the Polish by Renata Gorczynski, Benjamin Ivry, and C. K. Williams

MARY OLIVER
1935—

Nature is perfect, that is, perfectly functional and deserving admiration, "so long as you don't mind a little dying." Not a little, indeed, but only our consciousness knows that what a kingfisher knows is its only truth—hunger. Faced with a self-functioning order in which one creature serves as food to another, our consciousness renounces judgment. "I don't say he's right. Neither do I say he's wrong." Yet no action of ours is as efficient as the kingfisher's skill, submitted to instinct.

THE KINGFISHER

The kingfisher rises out of the black wave
like a blue flower, in his beak
he carries a silver leaf. I think this is
the prettiest world—so long as you don't mind
a little dying, how could there be a day in your whole life
that doesn't have its splash of happiness?
There are more fish than there are leaves
on a thousand trees, and anyway the kingfisher
wasn't born to think about it, or anything else.
When the wave snaps shut over his blue head, the water
remains water—hunger is the only story
he has ever heard in his life that he could believe.
I don't say he's right. Neither
do I say he's wrong. Religiously he swallows the silver leaf
with its broken red river, and with a rough and easy cry
I couldn't rouse out of my thoughtful body
if my life depended on it, he swings back
over the bright sea to do the same thing, to do it
(as I long to do something, anything) perfectly.

WISLAWA SZYMBORSKA
1923—

*We were taught that only man has an immortal soul. If today we speak differently
of a line separating us from the rest of living beings, does it mean that this line,
for us, doesn't exist? We feel it exists, and, using an old-fashioned expression, it
is due to the consciousness and free will of man. In other words, only we know
guilt, amidst the universal innocence of nature. And this is the subject of Wislawa
Szymborska's poem.*

IN PRAISE OF SELF-DEPRECATION

The buzzard has nothing to fault himself with.
Scruples are alien to the black panther.
Piranhas do not doubt the rightness of their actions.
The rattlesnake approves of himself without reservations.

The self-critical jackal does not exist.
The locust, alligator, trichina, horsefly
live as they live and are glad of it.

The killer-whale's heart weighs one hundred kilos
but in other respects it is light.

There is nothing more animal-like
than a clear conscience
on the third planet of the Sun.

Translated from the Polish by Magnus J. Krynski and Robert A. Maguire

A similar theme is treated in this poem: the self-torment afflicting us in the early morning.

FOUR IN THE MORNING

The hour from night to day.
The hour from side to side.
The hour for those past thirty.

The hour swept clean to the crowing of cocks.
The hour when earth betrays us.
The hour when wind blows from extinguished stars.
The hour of and-what-if-nothing-remains-after-us.

The hollow hour.
Blank, empty.
The very pit of all other hours.

No one feels good at four in the morning.
If ants feel good at four in the morning
—three cheers for the ants. And let five o'clock come
if we're to go on living.

Translated from the Polish by Magnus J. Krynski and Robert A. Maguire

THEODORE ROETHKE
1908—1963

Ecological poems began being written toward the end of this century, though the idea of protecting nature is much older. In the 1920s, as a twelve-year-old, I drew the map of my kingdom. It had only forests, no fields, and the only means of transportation allowed was canoes. The only inhabitants of my kingdom were lovers of nature with proper diplomas.

We are sensitive today to the destruction brought by man to nature. A poem by Theodore Roethke tries to capture the vague feeling of shame that probably has more than once visited the destroyers. Roethke was the son of a gardener, an owner of large greenhouses, and he often returns in his poetry to the country of his childhood.

MOSS-GATHERING

To loosen with all ten fingers held wide and limber
And lift up a patch, dark-green, the kind for lining cemetery
    baskets,
Thick and cushiony, like an old-fashioned doormat,
The crumbling small hollow sticks on the underside mixed with
    roots,
And wintergreen berries and leaves still stuck to the top,—
That was moss-gathering.
But something always went out of me when I dug loose those
    carpets
Of green, or plunged to my elbow in the spongy yellowish moss of
    the marshes:
And afterwards I always felt mean, jogging back over the logging
    road,
As if I had broken the natural order of things in that swampland;
Disturbed some rhythm, old and of vast importance,
By pulling off flesh from the living planet;
As if I had committed, against the whole scheme of life, a
    desecration.

DENISE LEVERTOV

1923—

On our planet, the presence of nature, the enchantment of being, and the feeling of transience all go together. Every day is precious because this earth goes through its seasons, and every season might be our last; every moment of meeting an earthly creature is unique, unrepeatable. As here, the frailty of a salamander reminds one of the frailty of our lives.

LIVING

The fire in leaf and grass
so green it seems
each summer the last summer.

The wind blowing, the leaves
shivering in the sun,
each day the last day.

A red salamander
so cold and so
easy to catch, dreamily

moves his delicate feet
and long tail. I hold
my hand open for him to go.

Each minute the last minute.

ROBERT FRANCIS
1901—1987

And if nature asks us to treat it with humor? If Winnie the Pooh, Piglet, and Rabbit and his friends-and-relations, if all that humanization is precisely what nature expects from us? In other words, perhaps we are unable to say—to tell her—anything, except ascribing to her sadness, smiles, ominousness, serenity? It is just or not, but we like some species and don't like others. And Robert Francis likes waxwings so well that he decided to become one in order to attain wisdom.

WAXWINGS

Four Tao philosophers as cedar waxwings
chat on a February berrybush
in sun, and I am one.

Such merriment and such sobriety—
the small wild fruit on the tall stalk—
was this not always my true style?

Above an elegance of snow, beneath
a silk-blue sky a brotherhood of four
birds. Can you mistake us?

To sun, to feast, and to converse
and all together—for this I have abandoned
all my other lives.

PHILIP LEVINE
1928—

I like Philip Levine's work, but I chose a poem which is not typical. And it seems to me I recognize here his garden in Fresno, California, where he has been a college professor for many years.

A SLEEPLESS NIGHT

April, and the last of the plum blossoms
scatters on the black grass
before dawn. The sycamore, the lime,
the struck pine inhale
the first pale hints of sky.
                              An iron day,
I think, yet it will come
dazzling, the light
rise from the belly of leaves and pour
burning from the cups
of poppies.
                The mockingbird squawks
from his perch, fidgets,
and settles back. The snail, awake
for good, trembles from his shell
and sets sail for China. My hand dances
in the memory of a million vanished stars.

A man has every place to lay his head.

ROBERT HASS
1941—

Is this a poem about nature? Yes, because it deals with the change of seasons. It's not difficult to place the countryside near San Francisco. Hass, co-translator of my poetry into English, is an essentially Californian poet. Here he was born, and here he works as a professor at Berkeley.

LATE SPRING

And then in mid-May the first morning of steady heat,

the morning, Leif says, when you wake up, put on shorts, and
that's it for the day,

when you pour coffee and walk outside, blinking in the sun.

Strawberries have appeared in the markets, and peaches will soon;

squid is so cheap in the fishstores you begin to consult Japanese
and Italian cookbooks for the various and ingenious ways of
preparing *ika* and *calamari*;

and because the light will enlarge your days, your dreams at night
will be as strange as the jars of octopus you saw once in a
fisherman's boat under the summer moon;

and after swimming, white wine; and the sharing of stories before
dinner is prolonged because the relations of the children in the
neighborhood have acquired village intensity and the stories take
longer telling;

and there are the nights when the fog rolls in that nobody likes—
hey, fog, the Miwok sang, who lived here first, you better go home,
pelican is beating your wife—

and after dark in the first cool hour, your children sleep so heavily
in their beds exhausted from play, it is a pleasure to watch them,

Leif does not move a muscle as he lies there; no, wait; it is Luke who lies there in his eight-year-old body,

Leif is taller than you are and he isn't home; when he is, his feet will extend past the end of the mattress, and Kristin is at the corner in the dark, talking to neighborhood boys;

things change; there is no need for this dream-compelled narration; the rhythm will keep me awake, changing.

ZBIGNIEW MACHEJ
1958—

I know a poem of a young Polish poet on summer, on wanderings of water from the depths of the earth upwards into the leaves and roots of fruit trees, and still further and higher, into the fluid of a cloud.

ORCHARDS IN JULY

Waters from cold springs
and glittering minerals
tirelessly wander.
Patient, unceasing,
they overcome granite, layers
of hungry gravel, iridescent
precincts of clay. If they abandon
themselves to the black
roots it's only to go
up, as high as possible
through wells hidden
under the bark of fruit trees. Through
the green touched with gray, of leaves,
fallen petals of white
flowers with rosy edges,
apples heavy with sweet redness
and their bitterish seeds.
O, waters from cold
springs and glittering
minerals! You are awaited
by a cirrus with a fluid,
sunny outline
and by an abyss of blue
which has been rinsed
in the just wind.

Translated by Czeslaw Milosz and Robert Hass

W. S. MERWIN
1927—

I don't know whether this fine poem expresses more than the inadequacy of our language before sunrises and sunsets. Perhaps we cannot do much without personifying. The sun behaves as a live being does, even a human being; its sunset is melancholy, "in the cold without friends," though without regrets because it worked well all the day long for people. Yet it believes "in nothing," which may mean too that it doesn't believe in its resurrection after the night. Why a stream? . . . Pursuing the light, the stream also is alive; it splashes on the stones, and this is its flute-playing. It will run all night long, till dawn. And so, as we try to describe the most ordinary dusk, the mythological transformation of phenomena into persons occurs. And it's no wonder that many people have given to planets, to the sea, to the rivers, to the streams, faces of smaller or bigger deities.

DUSK IN WINTER

The sun sets in the cold without friends
Without reproaches after all it has done for us
It goes down believing in nothing
When it is gone I hear the stream running after it
It has brought its flute it is a long way

D. H. LAWRENCE
1885—1930

D. H. Lawrence, in all his philosophy, turned against inhibitions invented by civilization to bind people and not to allow them to live in agreement with their inborn instincts. Thence such an importance is given to sex in his writing, because by getting rid of his inhibitions in this respect, "natural man" appears in all his nakedness. In the America of the 1960s, not without referring to that current of thought, a very amusing series of cartoons appeared with a hero by name Mr. Natural. Yet this poem of Lawrence's speaks, on the contrary, about the difficulty of merging with nature. A warm garden is like the garden of Eden, but in it Adam, looking at the butterfly, realizes that he cannot establish contact with it, and cannot warn it not to fly away to its perdition. Compared with the butterfly, he is nearly omniscient.

BUTTERFLY

Butterfly, the wind blows sea-ward, strong beyond the garden wall!
Butterfly, why do you settle on my shoe, and sip the dirt on my shoe,
Lifting your veined wings, lifting them? big white butterfly!

Already it is October, and the wind blows strong to the sea
from the hills where snow must have fallen, the wind is polished
            with snow.
Here in the garden, with red geraniums, it is warm, it is warm
but the wind blows strong to sea-ward, white butterfly, content on
            my shoe!

Will you go, will you go from my warm house?
Will you climb on your big soft wings, black-dotted,
as up an invisible rainbow, an arch
till the wind slides you sheer from the arch-crest
and in a strange level fluttering you go out to sea-ward, white speck!

Farewell, farewell, lost soul!
you have melted in the crystalline distance,
it is enough! I saw you vanish into air.

GARY SNYDER
1930 —

My guess is that inspirations from Zen Buddhism in Gary Snyder explain his gift
of attention. Much empathic attention is needed to meditate upon the fate of one
small living creature.

DRAGONFLY

Dragonfly
Dead on the snow
How did you come so high
Did you leave your seed child
In a mountain pool
Before you died

Evolution Basin IX 69

THEODORE ROETHKE
1908—1963

To describe a bird, an animal, a plant is difficult, because they elude that imperfect instrument which is our language. A pedantic description in textbooks of zoology or botany does not attempt to capture the very essence of a given species, but a poet likes to nail down something which is proper only to a given thing, be it "wolf-ishness," "elephantineness," "mapleness," or "carnationness." He makes use of comparisons: carnations have leaves like "Corinthian scrolls," and the chilly air is "hyacinthine." Though we are not sure that he succeeds, because a carnation does not mean the same thing to each one of us.

CARNATIONS

Pale blossoms, each balanced on a single jointed stem,
And leaves curled back in elaborate Corinthian scrolls;
And the air cool, as if drifting down from wet hemlocks,
Or rising out of ferns not far from water,
A crisp hyacinthine coolness,
Like that clear autumnal weather of eternity,
The windless perpetual morning above a September cloud.

ROBINSON JEFFERS
1887—1962

A foundation of admirers of Robinson Jeffers preserves as a relic his home in Carmel on the shores of the Pacific. When Jeffers and his wife, Una Custer, after the dramatic procedures of her divorce, first came to Carmel in 1914, it was a little village in the pine forests. Jeffers bought land and built their house by the sea from granite boulders, which he called Tor House. They lived there together until her death, and then he lived there until his death in 1962. Today the shore is completely built up, fortunately with one-family homes rather than high-rise buildings such as one finds on the shores of the Mediterranean in France and Spain. In this poem, Jeffers gives a short presentation of his philosophy, which he called "inhumanism." It advises inhumanization, that is, getting rid of human measurements, which deceive us because everything then refers to man, without whom the universe can perfectly exist. According to his philosophy, the human species, that destructive plasm on the surface of the globe, will disappear, and then everything will once again be perfectly beautiful.

CARMEL POINT

The extraordinary patience of things!
This beautiful place defaced with a crop of suburban houses—
How beautiful when we first beheld it,
Unbroken field of poppy and lupin walled with clean cliffs;
No instrusion but two or three horses pasturing,
Or a few milch cows rubbing their flanks on the outcrop rockheads—
Now the spoiler has come: does it care?
Not faintly. It has all time. It knows the people are a tide
That swells and in time will ebb, and all
Their works dissolve. Meanwhile the image of the pristine beauty
Lives in the very grain of the granite,
Safe as the endless ocean that climbs our cliff. — As for us:
We must uncenter our minds from ourselves;
We must unhumanize our views a little, and become confident
As the rock and ocean that we were made from.

GALWAY KINNELL
1927—

Perhaps poets of the twentieth century are busy making a catalog of all existing things. Here they have a good patron and predecessor, the omnivorous Walt Whitman. But it is interesting to note that in the very beginning of our century Rainer Maria Rilke—a poet, it would seem, of inner experiences—tried to describe things of the visible world in such poems as "The Panther," "Blue Hortense," "Archaic Torso of Apollo," "Persian Heliotrope," "Mountain," and "The Ball."

DAYBREAK

On the tidal mud, just before sunset,
dozens of starfishes
were creeping. It was
as though the mud were a sky
and enormous, imperfect stars
moved across it slowly
as the actual stars cross heaven.
All at once they stopped,
and as if they had simply
increased their receptivity
to gravity they sank down
into the mud; they faded down
into it and lay still; and by the time
pink of sunset broke across them
they were as invisible
as the true stars at daybreak.

D. H. LAWRENCE
1885—1930

MYSTIC

They call all experience of the senses *mystic,* when the experience
    is considered.
So an apple becomes *mystic* when I taste in it
the summer and the snows, the wild welter of earth
and the insistence of the sun.

All of which things I can surely taste in a good apple.
Though some apples taste preponderantly of water, wet and sour
and some of too much sun, brackish sweet
like lagoon-water, that has been too much sunned.

If I say I taste these things in an apple, I am called *mystic,* which
    means a liar.
The only way to eat an apple is to hog it down like a pig
and taste nothing
that is *real.*

But if I eat an apple, I like to eat it with all my senses awake.
Hogging it down like a pig I call the feeding of corpses.

ROBERT MORGAN
1944—

Some poets, concentrating their attention on the object, renounce the privileges of their "I," approaching the object cautiously, and even ascetically. Robert Morgan writes about things known to him in his childhood in a rural region of America. "Honey" is not unlike practical advice for a beekeeper.

HONEY

Only calmness will reassure
the bees to let you rob their hoard.
Any sweat of fear provokes them.
Approach with confidence, and from
the side, not shading their entrance.
And hush smoke gently from the spout
of the pot of rags, for sparks will
anger them. If you go near bees
every day they will know you.
And never jerk or turn so quick
you excite them. If weeds are trimmed
around the hive they have access
and feel free. When they taste your smoke
they fill themselves with honey and
are laden and lazy as you
lift the lid to let in daylight.
No bee full of sweetness wants to
sting. Resist greed. With the top off
you touch the fat gold frames, each cell
a hex perfect as a snowflake,
a sealed relic of sun and time
and roots of many acres fixed
in crystal-tight arrays, in rows
and lattices of sweeter latin
from scattered prose of meadow, woods.

JOANNE KYGER
1934—

A few words on a king. He doesn't know that he's a king; he's taciturn and a hermit. But the human imagination has adorned him with features proper to a monarch. He is also a sage, though he doesn't speak at all. He appears in innumerable fairy tales and legends. The bear doesn't visit European poetry anymore, but he quite often does American poetry, as in California poet Joanne Kyger. She belongs to the movement of the Beat Generation, studied at the University of California at Santa Barbara, practiced Zen, lived a couple of years in Japan, and now lives in Bolinas, California.

DESTRUCTION

First of all do you remember the way a bear goes through
a cabin when nobody is home? He goes through
the front door. I mean he really goes *through* it. Then
he takes the cupboard off the wall and eats a can of lard.

He eats all the apples, limes, dates, bottled decaffeinated
coffee, and 35 pounds of granola. The asparagus soup cans
fall to the floor. Yum! He chomps up Norwegian crackers
stashed for the winter. And the bouillon, salt, pepper,
paprika, garlic, onions, potatoes.

                    He rips the Green Tara
poster from the wall. Tries the Coleman Mustard. Spills
the ink, tracks in the flour. Goes up stairs and takes
a shit. Rips open the water bed, eats the incense and
drinks the perfume. Knocks over the Japanese tansu
and the Persian miniature of a man on horseback watching
a woman bathing.

            Knocks *Shelter. Whole Earth Catalogue,*
Planet Drum, Northern Mists, Truck Tracks, and
Women's Sports into the oozing water bed mess.

He goes
down stairs and out the back wall. He keeps on going
for a long way and finds a good cave to sleep it all off.
Luckily he ate the whole medicine cabinet, including stash
of LSD, Peyote, Psilocybin, Amanita, Benzedrine, Valium
and aspirin.

MARY OLIVER
1935—

In view of the great number of nihilizing experiences in literature of the twentieth century, one should appreciate wisdom drawn by people from their contact with nature. Those experiences cannot be rationally defined. But perhaps most essential is the feeling of a universal rhythmn of which we are a part simply thanks to the circulation of our blood. In this poem of Mary Oliver's, good and evil, guilt and despair, are proper to the human world, but beyond there is a larger world and its very existence calls us to transcend our human worries.

WILD GEESE

You do not have to be good.
You do not have to walk on your knees
for a hundred miles through the desert, repenting.
You only have to let the soft animal of your body
    love what it loves.
Tell me about despair, yours, and I will tell you mine.
Meanwhile the world goes on.
Meanwhile the sun and the clear pebbles of the rain
are moving across the landscapes,
over the prairies and the deep trees,
the mountains and the rivers.
Meanwhile the wild geese, high in the clean blue air,
are heading home again.
Whoever you are, no matter how lonely,
the world offers itself to your imagination,
calls to you like the wild geese, harsh and exciting—
over and over announcing your place
in the family of things.

WISLAWA SZYMBORSKA
1923 —

Szymborska's poetry is strongly influenced by modern science. She assumes that the borderline between us and the rest of nature is tenuous. On the other hand, she knows that our inveterate habits incline us to look at animals and insects with a feeling of our special privilege. Thence her ironic poem.

SEEN FROM ABOVE

On a dirt road lies a dead beetle.
Three little pairs of legs carefully folded on his belly.
Instead of death's chaos—neatness and order.
The horror of this sight is mitigated,
the range strictly local, from witchgrass to spearmint.
Sadness is not contagious.
The sky is blue.

For our peace of mind, their death seemingly shallower,
animals do not pass away, but simply die,
losing—we wish to believe—less of awareness and the world,
leaving—it seems to us—a stage less tragic.
Their humble little souls do not haunt our dreams,
they keep their distance,
know their place.

So here lies the dead beetle on the road,
glistens unlamented when the sun hits.
A glance at him is as good as a thought:
he looks as though nothing important had befallen him.
What's important is valid supposedly for us.
For just our life, for just our death,
a death that enjoys an extorted primacy.

Translated from the Polish by Magnus J. Krynski and Robert A. Maguire

JANE HIRSHFIELD
1953—

Young Prince Siddhartha, carefully protected by his parents from the knowledge that there exist illness and death, once escaped from his palace and in the streets of the city discovered suffering as the law of the world. A great compassion for all living creatures forced him to look for a means to liberate them. After years of ascetic contemplation he became a Buddha and gave rise to one of the great religions of humanity. This poem about a mother who would like to protect her child from unavoidable knowledge was written by a California poet, a Buddhist, and, besides, a person whom I number among my friends.

A STORY

A woman tells me
the story of a small wild bird,
beautiful on her window sill, dead three days.
How her daughter came suddenly running,
"It's moving, Mommy, he's alive."
And when she went, it was.
The emerald wing-feathers stirred, the throat
seemed to beat again with pulse.
Closer then, she saw how the true life lifted
under the wings. Turned her face
so her daughter would not see, though she would see.

JEAN FOLLAIN
1903—1971

FACE THE ANIMAL

It's not always easy
to face the animal
even if it looks at you
without fear or hate
it does so fixedly
and seems to disdain
the subtle secret it carries
it seems better to feel
the obviousness of the world
that noisily day and night
drills and damages
the silence of the soul.

Tanslated from the French by Heather McHugh

JORGE GUILLÉN
1893—1984

*Incarnating oneself in a bird: how many associations with mythology in the history
of poetry? Not only incarnation, but also feeling what a bird feels, an imagination
allowing us to do that. This poem by the Spanish poet Jorge Guillén has as its
subject the delight of existing, which we guess to be in all living beings because,
since it is not refused to us, it must be all the stronger when it is more spontaneous
and further from thinking.*

FLIGHT

Through summer air
The ascending gull
Dominates the expanse, the sea, the world
Under the blue, under clouds
Like the whitest wool-tufts,
And supreme, regal,
It soars.

All of space is a wave transfixed.

White and black feathers
Slow the ascent,
Suddenly slipping on the air,
On the vast light.

It buoys up the whiteness of the void.

And suspended, its wings abandon themselves
To clarity, to the transparent depths
Where flight, with stilled wings,
Subsists,
Gives itself entirely to its own delight, its falling,
And plunges into its own passing—
A pure instant of life.

Translated from the Spanish by Reginald Gibbons

EMILY DICKINSON
1830—1886

A NARROW FELLOW IN THE GRASS

A narrow Fellow in the Grass
Occasionally rides—
You may have met Him—did you not
His notice sudden is—

the Grass divides as with a Comb—
A spotted shaft is seen—
And then it closes at your feet
And opens further on—

He likes a Boggy Acre
A Floor too cool for Corn—
Yet when a Boy, and Barefoot—
I more than once at Noon
Have passed, I thought, a Whip lash
Unbraiding in the Sun
When stooping to secure it
It wrinkled, and was gone—

Several of Nature's People
I know, and they know me—
I feel for them a transport
Of cordiality—

But never met this Fellow
Attended, or alone
Without a tighter breathing
And Zero at the Bone—

ROBERT FROST
1874—1963

THE MOST OF IT

He thought he kept the universe alone;
For all the voice in answer he could wake
Was but the mocking echo of his own
From some tree-hidden cliff across the lake.
Some morning from the boulder-broken beach
He would cry out on life, that what it wants
Is not its own love back in copy speech,
But counter-love, original response.
And nothing ever came of what he cried
Unless it was the embodiment that crashed
In the cliff's talus on the other side,
And then in the far-distant water splashed,
But after time allowed for it to swim,
Instead of proving human when it neared
And someone else additional to him,
As a great buck it powerfully appeared,
Pushing the crumpled water up ahead,
And landed pouring like a waterfall,
And stumbled through the rocks with horny tread,
And forced the underbrush—and that was all.

ANNA SWIR
1909—1984

THE SEA AND THE MAN

You will not tame this sea
either by humility or rapture.
But you can laugh
in its face.

Laughter
was invented by those
who live briefly
as a burst of laughter.

The eternal sea
will never learn to laugh.

Translated from the Polish by Czeslaw Milosz and Leonard Nathan

The Secret of a Thing

Poetry has always described things surrounding us, but as if inadvertently, swerving for a moment from the main topic, for instance, from the military action in the *Iliad*, to present in detail Achilles' shield. In European painting, an originally supplementary detail eventually becomes autonomous: the landscape, at first used as a background, became a *paysage;* dishes, meats, fruit, all that accompanies people, filling their tables, changed into "still lifes," a genre which attained its highest achievements probably in the seventeenth century by Dutch masters, in the eighteenth century by Chardin, and in the twentieth century by Cézanne.

In modernism there is much fascination with the object, and our changing attitude toward poets of the past seems to be connected with a shifting focus of attention. It is possible that the influence of the poets of old China and old Japan has contributed to the new awareness. That influence is already visible by the beginning of this century, in American imagism.

The modern poet has discovered how difficult it is to describe a thing, giving it center stage, withdrawing himself or herself, "objectivizing," for every one of us is bound to it by emotional ties inherited together with the language; our very vocabulary resists a detached contemplation. When the Japanese poet Bashō advised a poet describing a pine to learn from the pine, he wanted to say that contemplation of a thing—a reverent and pious approach to it—is a prerequisite of true art.

WALT WHITMAN
1819—1892

The strong presence of a thing described means that the poet believes in its real existence. That is the meaning of a programmatic and unfinished poem by Walt Whitman, "I Am the Poet," which rehabilitates a "naive" approach and rejects philosophy's unfavorable opinion on the direct testimony of our senses.

I AM THE POET

I am the poet of reality
I say the earth is not an echo
Nor man an apparition;
But that all the things seen are real,
The witness and albic dawn of things equally real
I have split the earth and the hard coal and rocks and the solid bed
    of the sea
And went down to reconnoitre there a long time,
And bring back a report,
And I understand that those are positive and dense every one
And that what they seem to the child they are
[And that the world is not joke,
Nor any part of it a sham].

WILLIAM BLAKE
1757—1827

William Blake had not, whatever his critics might have said, the mentality of a medieval peasant. He quarreled with his contemporaries, extolling the value of direct, naive perceptions, as opposed to images suggested by scientific theory. In defending the flat earth, he wanted to say that its image is better adapted to human needs than the image of an earth-ball, one of the planetary bodies.

FROM "MILTON"

And every Space that a Man views around his dwelling-place
Standing on his own roof or in his garden on a mount
Of twenty-five cubits in height, such space is his Universe:
And on its verge the Sun rises & sets, the Clouds bow
To meet the flat Earth & the Sea in such an order'd Space:
The Starry heavens reach no further, but here bend and set
On all sides, & the two Poles turn on their valves of gold;
And if he move his dwelling-place, his heavens also move
Where'er he goes, & all his neighbourhood bewail his loss.
Such are the Spaces called Earth & such its dimension.
As to that false appearance which appears to the reasoner
As of a Globe rolling thro' Voidness, it is a delusion of Ulro.

WALT WHITMAN
1819—1892

THE RUNNER

On a flat road runs the well-train'd runner,
He is lean and sinewy with muscular legs,
He is thinly clothed, he leans forward as he runs,
With lightly closed fists and arms partially rais'd.

A FARM PICTURE

Through the ample open door of the peaceful country barn,
A sunlit pasture filled with cattle and horses feeding,
And haze and vista, and the far horizon fading away.

The affinity between painting and poetry was strongly stressed in ancient Chinese poetry, and often a poet and a painter filled a scroll of paper together. But in the Western world also, poetry was early compared to painting, and Horace said "Ut pictura poesis" (In poetry, as in painting).

ON A PAINTING BY WANG THE CLERK OF YEN LING

The slender bamboo is like a hermit.
The simple flower is like a maiden.
The sparrow tilts on the branch.
A gust of rain sprinkles the flowers.
He spreads his wings to fly
And shakes all the leaves.
The bees gathering honey
Are trapped in the nectar.
What a wonderful talent
That can create an entire Spring
With a brush and a sheet of paper.
If he would try poetry
I know he would be a master of words.

Translated from the Chinese by Kenneth Rexroth

ROBERT MORGAN
1944-

Robert Morgan's ambition is to describe objects in a matter-of-fact manner. And he finds his material in the countryside and small towns of the American South.

BELLROPE

The line through the hold in the dank
vestibule ceiling ended in
a powerful knot worn slick, swinging
in the breeze from those passing. Half
an hour before service Uncle
Allen pulled the call to worship,
hauling down the rope like the starting
cord of a motor, and the tower
answered and answered, fading
as the clapper lolled aside. I watched
him before Sunday school heave on
the line as on a wellrope. And
the wheel creaked up there as heavy
buckets emptied out their startle
and spread a cold splash to farthest
coves and hollows, then sucked the rope
back into the loft, leaving just
the knot within reach, trembling
with its high connections.

JUDAH AL-HARIZI

c. 1170—1235

But let us move back to the middle ages. In Spain, Toledo was, at that time, a known center of writing in Hebrew, and there was born the poet Al-Harizi, author of the slightly jocular quatrains that I include here.

THE LIGHTNING

And the lightning laughs at the clouds,
like a warrior who runs without growing weary or faint.

Or like a night watchman who dozes off,
then opens one eye for an instant, and shuts it.

Translated from the Hebrew by T. Carmi

THE SUN

Look: the sun has spread its wings
over the earth to dispel the darkness.

Like a great tree, with its roots in heaven,
and its branches reaching down to the earth.

Translated from the Hebrew by T. Carmi

THE LUTE

Look: the lute sounds in the girl's arms,
delighting the heart with its beautiful voice.

Like a baby crying in his mother's arms,
while she sings and laughs as he cries.

Translated from the Hebrew by T. Carmi

ROBINSON JEFFERS
1887—1962

Poems, as realistically descriptive as possible, occasionally engage in polemics with those who might question the choice of topic, as, for instance, in this poem of Robinson Jeffers.

BOATS IN FOG

Sports and gallantries, the stage, the arts, the antics of dancers,
The exuberant voices of music,
Have charm for children but lack nobility; it is bitter
   earnestness
That makes beauty; the mind
Knows, grown adult.
                  A sudden fog-drift muffled the ocean,
A throbbing of engines moved in it,
At length, a stone's throw out, between the rocks and the
   vapor,
One by one moved shadows
Out of the mystery, shadows, fishing-boats, trailing each other
Following the cliff for guidance,
Holding a difficult path between the peril of the sea-fog
And the foam on the shore granite.
One by one, trailing their leader, six crept by me,
Out of the vapor and into it,
The throb of their engines subdued by the fog, patient and
   cautious,
Coasting all round the peninsula
Back to the buoys in Monterey harbor. A flight of pelicans
Is nothing lovelier to look at;
The flight of the planets is nothing nobler; all the arts lose
   virtue
Against the essential reality
Of creatures going about their business among the equally
Earnest elements of nature.

EVENING EBB

The ocean has not been so quiet for a long while; five night-
    herons
Fly shorelong voiceless in the hush of the air
Over the calm of an ebb that almost mirrors their wings.
The sun has gone down, and the water has gone down
From the weed-clad rock, but the distant cloud-wall rises. The ebb
    whispers.
Great cloud-shadows float in the opal water.
Through rifts in the screen of the world pale gold gleams, and the
    evening
Star suddenly glides like a flying torch.
As if we had not been meant to see her; rehearsing behind
The screen of the world for another audience.

ROBERT HASS
1941—

Robert Hass, like Jeffers, is a California poet. In this poem, an object (clay figurine) and a typical California landscape are given simultaneously.

THE IMAGE

The child brought blue clay from the creek
and the woman made two figures: a lady and a deer.
At that season deer came down from the mountain
and fed quietly in the redwood canyons.
The woman and the child regarded the figure of the lady,
the crude roundnesses, the grace, the coloring like shadow.
They were not sure where she came from,
except the child's fetching and the woman's hands
and the lead-blue clay of the creek
where the deer sometimes showed themselves at sundown.

ROLF JACOBSEN
1907—

Colors are the most essential qualities of things, not lines. Since Cézanne so believed,
he admired the Renaissance painting of Venice, because of its luxuriance of color.
In Norwegian poet Rolf Jacobsen, colors—as they are of feminine gender—are
a feminine part of nature, and are treated as women. For him, Crimson is "she,"
and Cobalt, too, is "she."

COBALT

Colors are words' little sisters. They can't become soldiers.
I've loved them secretly for a long time.
They have to stay home and hang up the sheer curtains
in our ordinary bedroom, kitchen and alcove.

I'm very close to young Crimson, and brown Sienna
but even closer to thoughtful Cobalt with her distant eyes and
         untrampled spirit.
We walk in dew.
The night sky and the southern oceans
are her possessions
and a tear-shaped pendant on her forehead:
the pearls of Cassiopeia.
We walk in dew on late nights.

But the others.
Meet them on a June morning at four o'clock
when they come rushing toward you,
on your way to a morning swim in the green cove's spray.
Then you can sunbathe with them on the smooth rocks.
       —Which one will you make yours?

Translated from the Norwegian by Roger Greenwald

WALLACE STEVENS
1879—1955

Wallace Stevens was under the spell of science and scientific methods. An analytical tendency is visible in his poems on reality, and this is just opposite to the advice of Zen poet Bashō, who wanted to capture the thing in a single stroke. When Stevens tries to describe two pears, as if for an inhabitant of another planet, he enumerates one after another their chief qualities, making his analysis akin to a Cubist painting. But pears prove to be impossible to describe.

STUDY OF TWO PEARS

I

Opusculum paedagogum.
The pears are not viols,
Nudes or bottles.
They resemble nothing else.

2

They are yellow forms
Composed of curves
Bulging toward the base.
They are touched red.

3

They are not flat surfaces
Having curved outlines.
They are round
Tapering toward the top.

4

In the way they are modelled
There are bits of blue.
A hard dry leaf hangs
From the stem.

5

The yellow glistens.
It glistens with various yellows,
Citrons, oranges and greens
Flowering over the skin.

6

The shadows of the pears
Are blobs on the green cloth.
The pears are not seen
As the observer wills.

WILLIAM CARLOS WILLIAMS
1883—1963

The Objectivists, active in New York in the 1920s, left a durable trace on American poetry; the poem "The Red Wheelbarrow" by William Carlos Williams, who for a time was one of them, is a classic that must not be omitted from my collection. Maybe in this poem all his warmth and compassion are hardly signalled, but the poem is important.

THE RED WHEELBARROW

So much depends
upon

a red wheel
barrow

glazed with rain
water

beside the white
chickens.

WISLAWA SZYMBORSKA
1923 —

Poetry in the twentieth century has been moving, in at least one of its branches,
toward the philosophical essay, and this has gone along with a certain blurring of
borderlines between literary genres. If abstraction is dangerous to poetry, this ten-
dency nevertheless contributes to its ability to ask some basic questions about the
structure of the universe. A poem by Wislawa Szymborska opposes the human (i.e.,
language) to the inanimate world and shows that our understanding of it is illusory.
Personally, I think that she is too scientific and that we are not so separated from
things.

VIEW WITH A GRAIN OF SAND

We call it a grain of sand
but it calls itself neither grain nor sand.
It does just fine without a name,
whether general, particular,
permanent, passing,
incorrect or apt.

Our glance, our touch mean nothing to it.
It doesn't feel itself seen and touched.
And that it fell on the windowsill
is only our experience, not its.
For it it's no different than falling on anything else
with no assurance that it's finished falling
or that it's falling still.

The window has a wonderful view of a lake
but the view doesn't view itself.
It exists in this world
colorless, shapeless,
soundless, odorless, and painless.

The lake's floor exists floorlessly
and its shore exists shorelessly.

Its water feels itself neither wet nor dry
and its waves to themselves are neither singular nor plural.
They splash deaf to their own noise
on pebbles neither large nor small.

And all this beneath a sky by nature skyless
in which the sun sets without setting at all
and hides without hiding behind an unminding cloud.
The wind ruffles it, its only reason being
that it blows.

A second passes.
A second second.
A third.
But they're three seconds only for us.

Time has passed like a courier with urgent news.
But that's just our simile.
The character's invented, his haste is make-believe,
his news inhuman.

Translated from the Polish by Stanislaw Barańczak and Clara Cavanagh

FRANCIS PONGE
1899—1988

Francis Ponge, a rationalist in the Cartesian tradition, wrote "objeu" (objet-jeu—object-play) poems, in which things provided him an opportunity for linguistic games. I suspect he wrote less about visible phenomena than about their adventures within the dictionary of the French language.

THE FROG

When little matchsticks of rain bounce off drenched fields, an amphibian dwarf, a maimed Ophelia, barely the size of a fist, sometimes hops under the poet's feet and flings herself into the next pond.

Let the nervous little thing run away. She has lovely legs. Her whole body is sheathed in waterproof skin. Hardly meat, her long muscles have an elegance neither fish nor fowl. But to escape one's fingers, the virtue of fluidity joins forces with her struggle for life. Goitrous, she starts panting. . . . And that pounding heart, those wrinkled eyelids, that drooping mouth, move me to let her go.

Translated from the French by Beth Archer

ALEKSANDER WAT

1900—1967

Looking at a painting is like second-degree contemplation, entering into cooperation
with the painter who had seen and admired the colors of the object.

FACING BONNARD

Blond light blew away grayness, shadows, mists,
from a body that left the bathtub and does not yet go to the
    coffin.
The body is tawny, flame-spotted, and the bathtub, rosy,
    flesh-colored.
And the coffin? As usual with a coffin: dimly purple.
(Besides, the coffin's not visible: its colors suffice).

That translation from our world, don't ask whether faithful,
gives pleasure to the eye. The other senses are mum.
But to the eye it gives pleasure. That's enough. Quite.
Be patient. Wait. You will see how that pleasure
opens up as an egg of dream-meditation.
Our artist enclosed in it a ballet of possibilities
where he himself—and you—are both an observer and an author,
a corps de ballet, surely, but also a true soloist.

Translated from the Polish by Czeslaw Milosz and Leonard Nathan

MUSO SOSEKI

1275—1351

It is amazing to what extent the mountain appears and reappears in poetry of various languages, beginning of course with the Bible, as a sacred presence to be contemplated. Often its autonomous existence is opposed to the passing states of mind and feelings of a human being.

MAGNIFICENT PEAK

By its own nature
   it towers above
      the tangle of rivers
Don't say
   it's a lot of dirt
      piled high
Without end the mist of dawn
   the evening cloud
      draw their shadows across it
From the four directions
   you can look up and see it
      green and steep and wild.

Translated from the Japanese by W. S. Merwin

DENISE LEVERTOV
1923—

WITNESS

Sometimes the mountain
is hidden from me in veils
of cloud, sometimes
I am hidden from the mountain
in veils of inattention, apathy, fatigue,
when I forget or refuse to go
down to the shore or a few yards
up the road, on a clear day,
to reconfirm
that witnessing presence.

Travel

In old Arabic poetry love, song, blood, and travel appear as four basic desires of the human heart and the only effective means against our fear of death. Thus travel is elevated to the dignity of the elementary needs of humankind. "To sail is necessary, to live is not" *(Navigare est necesse, vivere non est necesse)*—these words were, according to Plutarch, pronounced by a Roman before the departure of a ship in tempestuous weather. Whatever practical reasons push people out of their homes to seek adventure, travel undoubtedly removes us from familiar sights and from everyday routine. It offers to us a pristine world seen for the first time and is a powerful means of inducing wonder. And since poetry is an expression of wondering at things, landscapes, people, their habits and mores, poetry and travel are allied.

Man has always travelled, yet the great mass of humanity remained sedentary, and only since the beginning of the twentieth century have we witnessed the new phenomenon: tourism. Fast international express trains and transatlantic steamers were greeted by poets as the implementation of modernity and of a new cosmopolitan spirit. The buoyant mood of the period just preceding World War I, called in France "La Belle Epoque," is present in French poets such as Valery Larbaud and Blaise Cendrars. Larbaud invented a figure of an international traveller, a millionaire, Barnabooth, and published his presumed poems in 1908. Cendrars (in reality a Swiss, born Ferdinand Sauser) drew the images of his largely descriptive poems from both America and Russia. In 1912 he published his famous poem "Easter in New York," as important for modern poetry as is "Zone," by his friend Guillaume Apollinaire. In 1913 he wrote his long poem entitled "Prose of the

Transsiberian Railway and of little Jeanne of France." His postwar poems were snapshots from different continents, often collages.

Travel provided one of the main topics for old Chinese poetry, but it was not international. The huge size of the Empire gave much opportunity to discover the unfamiliar and the exotic within its borders. These were journeys by land, often to remote provinces.

I have selected several poems about the train, because it has stirred the imagination of poets (beginning with Walt Whitman's in "To a Locomotive in Winter"). The train means a deployment of sights and people beyond the window, but often acquires sinister traits.

Of course, I could not omit poems dealing with the most ancient way of travelling—by foot.

VALERY LARBAUD
1881—1957

IMAGES

1

One day in a popular quarter of Kharkov,
(O that southern Russia where all the women
With white-shawled heads look so like Madonnas!)
I saw a young woman returning from the fountain,
Bearing, Russian-style, as Roman women did in the time of Ovid,
Two pails suspended from the ends of a wooden
Yoke balanced on neck and shoulders.
And I saw a child in rags approach and speak to her.
Then, bending her body lovingly to the right,
She moved so the pail of pure water touched the cobblestone
Level with the lips of the child who had kneeled to drink.

2

One morning, in Rotterdam, on Boompjes quai
(It was September 18, 1900, around eight o'clock),
I observed two young ladies on their way to work;
Opposite one of the great iron bridges, they said farewell,
Their paths diverging.
Tenderly they embraced; their trembling hands
Wanted, but did not want, to part; their mouths
Withdrew sadly and came together again soon again
While they gazed fixedly into each other's eyes . . .
They stood thus for a long moment side by side,
Straight and still amid the busy throng,
While the tugboats rumbled by on the river,
And the whistling trains maneuvered on the iron bridges.

3

Between Cordova and Seville
Is a little station where the South Express,
For no apparent reason, always stops.

In vain the traveler looks for a village
Beyond the station asleep under the eucalyptus:
He sees but the Andalusian countryside: green and golden.
But across the way, on the other side of the track,
Is a hut made of black boughs and clay,
From which, at the sound of the rain, ragged children swarm forth,
The eldest sister, leading them, comes forward on the platform
And, smiling, without uttering a word,
Dances for pennies.
Her feet in the heavy dust look black;
Her dark, filthy face is devoid of beauty;
She dances, and through the large holes of her ash-gray skirt,
One can see the agitation of her thin, naked thighs,
And the roll of her little yellow belly;
At the sight of which a few gentlemen,
Amid an aroma of cigars, chuckle obscenely in the dining car.

Post-Scriptum

O Lord, will it never be possible for me
To know the sweet woman, there in Southern Russia,
And those two young friends in Rotterdam,
And the young Andalusian beggar
And join with them
In an indissoluble friendship?
(Alas, they will not read these poems,
They will know neither my name, nor the feeling in my heart;
And yet they exist; they live now).
Will it never be possible for me to experience the great joy
Of knowing them?
For some strange reason, Lord, I feel that with those four
I should conquer a whole world!

Translated from the French by William Jay Smith

BLAISE CENDRARS
1887—1961

ALEUTIAN ISLANDS

1

High Cliffs lashed by icy polar winds
In the center of lush meadows
Reindeer elks musk-oxen
The Arctic foxes the beavers
Brooks swarming with fish
A low beach has been prepared to breed fur seals
On top of the cliff are collected the eider's nests
Its feathers are worth a real fortune.

2

Large and sturdy buildings which shelter a
        considerable number of traders
All around a small garden where all vegetation
        able to withstand the severe climate has
        been brought together
mountain ash pine trees Arctic willows
Bed of heather and Alpine plants

3

Bay spiked with rocky islets
In groups of five or six the seals bask in the sun
Or stretching out on the sand
They play together howling in that kind of hoarse tone
        that sounds like a dog's bark
Next to the Eskimos' hut is a shed where
        the skins are treated

Translated from the French by Monique Chefdor

FISH COVE

The water is so clear and so calm
Deep at the bottom you can see the white bushes
    of coral
The prismatic sway of hanging jellyfish
The yellow pink lilac fish taking flight
And at the foot of the wavy seaweeds the azure
    sea cucumbers and the urchins green and purple

Translated from the French by Monique Chefdor

HARVEST

A six-cylinder car and two Fords in the middle of
    the fields
In every direction as far as the horizon the slightly
    slanting swaths crisscross in a wavering
    diamond-shaped checkerboard pattern
Not a tree
From the North comes down the rumble and rattle of the
    automotive thrasher and forage wagon
And from the south come twelve empty trains to
    pick up the wheat

Translated from the French by Monique Chefdor

SOUTH

1. Tampa

The train has just come to a stop
Only two travelers get off on this scorching
    late summer morning
Both wear khaki suits and cork helmets
Both are followed by a black servant
    who carries their luggage
Both glance in the same casual way at the houses
    that are too white at the sky that is too blue
You can see the wind raise whirls of dust and the flies
    buzzing around the two mules of the only cab
The cabman is asleep the mouth wide open

Translated from the French by Monique Chefdor

FRISCO-CITY

It is an antique carcass eaten up by rust
The engine repaired twenty times does not make
    more than 7 to 8 knots
Besides to save expenses cinders and coal waste
    are its only fuel
Makeshift sails are hoisted whenever there is
    a fair wind
With his ruddy face his bushy eyebrows his pimply nose
    Master Hopkins is a true sailor
Small silver rings hang from his pierced ears
The ship's cargo is exclusively coffins of Chinese
    who died in America and wished to be buried
    in their homeland
Oblong boxes painted red or light blue or covered
    with golden characters
Just the type of merchandise it is illegal to ship

Translated from the French by Monique Chefdor

LI PO
701—762

Sometimes it is enough to climb a nearby mountain to see all human affairs literally from above, as is done by this great poet of the T'ang Dynasty, the Golden Age of Chinese poetry.

ANCIENT AIR

Climbed high, to gaze upon the sea,
Heaven and Earth, so vast, so vast.
Frost clothes all things in Autumn,
Winds waft, the broad wastes cold.
Glory, splendor; eastward flowing stream,
This world's affairs, just waves.
White sun covered, its dying rays,
The floating clouds, no resting place.
In lofty Wu-t'ung trees nest lowly finches.
Down among the thorny brush the Phoenix perches.
All that's left, to go home again,
Hand on my sword I sing, "The Going's Hard."

Translated from the Chinese by J. P. Seaton

CHANG CHI
768—830

When traveling, looking for a place to spend the night, we sometimes arrive at a spot we wouldn't otherwise ever have seen, as in the following poem by a Chinese poet.

COMING AT NIGHT TO A FISHERMAN'S HUT

Fisherman's hut, by the mouth of the river,
Water of the lake to his brushwood gate.
The traveler would beg night's lodging,
But the master's not yet home.
The bamboo thick, the village far.
Moon rises, fishing boats are few.
There! far off, along the sandy shore
The spring breeze moving his cloak of straw.

Translated from the Chinese by J. P. Seaton

PO CHÜ-I
772—846

And here travel at night, before dawn, in a horse carriage, obviously only one stretch of a longer journey—it associates in my mind with similar travels in my childhood when automobiles in my remote corner of Europe were few. I love Po Chü-I for the extraordinary vividness of his images.

STARTING EARLY

Washed by the rain, dust and grime are laid;
Skirting the river, the road's course is flat.
The moon has risen on the last remnants of night;
The travellers' speed profits by the early cold.
In the great silence I whisper a faint song;
In the black darkness are bred somber thoughts.
On the lotus-bank hovers a dewy breeze;
Through the rice furrows trickles a singing stream.
At the noise of our bells a sleeping dog stirs;
At the sight of our torches a roosting bird wakes.
Dawn glimmers through the shapes of misty trees . . .
For ten miles, till day at last breaks.

Translated from the Chinese by Arthur Waley

Po Chü-I is also the author of a poem of another kind of travel—travel in dreams.

A DREAM OF MOUNTAINEERING

At night, in my dream, I stoutly climbed a mountain,
Going out alone with my staff of holly-wood.
A thousand crags, a hundred hundred valleys—
In my dream-journey none were unexplored
And all the while my feet never grew tired
And my step was as strong as in my young days.
Can it be that when the mind travels backward
The body also returns to its old state?
And can it be, as between body and soul,
That the body may languish, while the soul is still strong?
Soul and body—both are vanities;
Dreaming and waking—both alike unreal.
In the day my feet are palsied and tottering;
In the night my steps go striding over the hills.
As day and night are divided in equal parts—
Between the two, I *get* as much as I *lose*.

Translated from the Chinese by Arthur Waley

LI PO

701—762

*It is somewhat surprising that this dramatic poem is the work of a Chinese poet.
In Western poetry, dreams of ascending are quite common because they refer to the
vertical structure of the Western religious world. No wonder that Dante ascends to
Paradise. But here we have a flight upward, following a goddess in a multicolored
robe, and, in contrast, the sudden sight of the earth below, the poor earth of
misfortune, after an invasion.*

ANCIENT AIR

Westward over Lotus Mountain
Afar, far off: Bright Star!
Hibiscus blooms in her white hand,
With airy step she climbs Great Purity.
Rainbow robes, trailing a broad sash,
Floating she brushes the heavenly stairs,
And invites me to mount the Cloud Terrace,
There to salute the immortal Wei Shu-ch'ing.
Ravished, mad, I go with her,
Upon a swan to reach the Purple Vault.
There I looked down, on Loyang's waters:
Vast sea of barbarian soldiers marching,
Fresh blood spattered on the grasses of the wilds.
Wolves, with men's hats on their heads.

Translated from the Chinese by J. P. Seaton

WANG WEI

701—761

War against peoples pressing out from the center of the Asiatic continent fills a considerable part of Chinese history. The travels of soldiers or officials sent to the "outskirts" are the frequent subject of poems. A whole cycle of such travel poems was written by a famous painter and poet, Wang Wei. He was a poet of Taoist and Buddhist inspiration, but he pursued the career of an official as well, albeit somewhat unwillingly, travelling through the vast spaces of the borderland territory.

SONG OF MARCHING WITH THE ARMY

Horns blow the travelers into movement.
Noisily they get under way with the sad sound
of reed pipes and chaos of neighing horses
as everyone struggles to ford Gold River.
The border sun settles in the desert
while sounds of war rise in smoke and dust.
We'll bind the neck of every chieftain
and bring them as presents for the emperor.

Translated from the Chinese by Tony and Willis Barnstone and Xu Haixin

As far as I know, among the translators of this poem there is a controversy as to the name of the bird shot by the hunter's arrow. Some opt for the vulture and some for the eagle. Apparently, in Chinese the same word is used for both. Of course I am not competent to take a position.

WATCHING THE HUNT

Strong wind. The horn-bow sings.
The generals are hunting in Wei Cheng.

In withered grass, the falcon's eye is sharper.
In melting snow, horse hooves are light.

They've just passed New Harvest Market
yet are already home at Willow Branch.

They look back. They shot the vulture
in a thousand miles of twilight clouds.

Translated from the Chinese by Tony and Willis Barnstone and Xu Haixin

CHANG YANG-HAO
1269—1329

Several centuries have passed since Wang Wei was writing his poems. We are now in a different period of Chinese history, and the reflection on time's passing makes an integral part of this poem—a poem like the Bible's vanity of vanities, with two magnificent concluding lines.

RECALLING THE PAST AT T'UNG PASS

As if gathered together,
     the peaks of the ranges.
As if raging,
   the waves on these banks.
Winding along
    these mountains & rivers,
the road to the T'ung Pass.
I look west
   & hesitant I lament
here where
   opposing armies passed through.
Palaces
  of countless rulers
  now but dust.
Empires rise:
   people suffer.
Empires fall:
   people suffer.

"Made new" by C. H. Knock and G. G. Gach

ROLF JACOBSEN
1907—

*There is no reason to stay with Chinese poetry, so I return to the twentieth century
and to train travel. Very often, the train is presented as the site of observation by
a person who travels. Beyond, out the window, there are towns, cities, and in this
case a Norwegian landscape of villages, provoking a philosophical reflection on the
life of their inhabitants, life deprived of love, unfulfilled, with an enormous potential
which waits for liberation.*

EXPRESS TRAIN

Express train 1256 races alongside hidden, remote villages. House
after house wanders by, pale gray, shivering. Rail fences, rocks and
lakes, and the closed gates.

 Then I have to think in the morning twilight: What would
happen if someone could release the loneliness of those hearts?
People live there, no one can see them, they walk across rooms,
in behind the doors, the need, blank-eyed, hardened by love they
cannot give and no one gets a chance to give them. What would
rise higher here than the mountains—the Skarvang Hills—what
flame, what force, what storms of steady light?

Express train 1256, eight soot-black cars, turns toward new, endlessly
unknown villages. Springs of light behind the panes, unseen wells
of power along the mountains—these we travel past, hurry past,
only four minutes late for Marnardal.

Translated from the Norwegian by Roger Greenwald

ANTONIO MACHADO
1899—1939

A train compartment, not necessarily what is seen moving beyond the window, may appear as the background, with fellow passengers as the object of attention, and speculation about their internal world—thoughts, dreams. Nevertheless, the duality of motion internal and external seems to be important. Antonio Machado places his characters in a night train; the visibility of what's outside is limited. "A traveler mad with grief" and the narrator both are busy with their reminiscences. Unexpectedly, the end is like an epiphany.

RAINBOW AT NIGHT
for Don Ramón del Valle-Inclán

    The train moves through the Guadarrama
one night on the way to Madrid.
The moon and the fog create
high up a rainbow.
Oh April moon, so calm,
driving up the white clouds!

    The mother holds her boy
sleeping on her lap.
The boy sleeps, and nevertheless
sees the green fields outside,
and trees lit up by sun,
and the golden butterflies.

    The mother, her forehead dark
between a day gone and a day to come,
sees a fire nearly out
and an oven with spiders.

    There's a traveler mad with grief,
no doubt seeing odd things;
he talks to himself, and when he looks
wipes us out with his look.

I remember fields under snow,
and pine trees of other mountains.

And you, Lord, through whom we all
have eyes, and who sees souls,
tell us if we all one
day will see your face.

Translated from the Spanish by Robert Bly

WILLIAM STAFFORD
1914—1993

Until recently, the train symbolized any travel, and that's why poets wrote so much about it. They were fascinated by landscapes, scenes moving beyond the window— mysterious because seen only for an instant. And so for William Stafford, a group of Indians out the window of the dining car reveals itself as the Other, with its own sequence of events (a funeral), which, for a short time only, crosses the sequence inside.

VACATION

One scene as I bow to pour her coffee:—

    Three Indians in the scouring drouth
    huddle at the grave scooped in the gravel,
    lean to the wind as our train goes by.
    Someone is gone.
    There is dust on everything in Nevada.

I pour the cream.

JOHN HAINES
1924—

Here again a window, and the filling of the immensity of space, mostly deserted,
as a typical feature of the American continent. It is the north we nearly see, the
stern and miserly light above a certain geographical latitude. The settlement is
really a camp by a mine, and there is the hint of a complete barrier between the
white observer and the Indian tribe.

THE TRAIN STOPS AT HEALY FORK

We pressed our faces
against the freezing glass,
saw the red soil
mixed with snow,
and a strand of barbed wire.

A line of boxcars
stood open on a siding,
their doorways
briefly afire in the sunset.

We saw the scattered iron
and timber of the campsite,
the coal seam
in the river bluff,
the twilight green of the icefall.

But the coppery tribesmen
we looked for had vanished,
the children of wind and shadow,
gone off with their rags
and hunger
to the blue edge of night.

Our train began to move,
bearing north,
sounding its hoarse whistle
in the starry gloom of the canyon.

BRONISLAW MAJ
1953—

A very different landscape makes its appearance beyond the window in a poem by
Bronislaw Maj: autumn countryside in Poland (mist, newly plowed earth, women
in dark shawls), but here too the Other calls for reconstructing some common story,
and for retaining it in memory because this image is given only once.

SEEN FLEETINGLY, FROM A TRAIN

Seen fleetingly, from a train:
a foggy evening, strands of smoke
hanging immobile over fields,
the humid blackness of earth, the sun
almost set—against its fading shield,
far away, two dots: women in dark wraps
coming back from church perhaps, perhaps
one tells something to another, some common story,
of sinful lives perhaps—her words
distinct and simple but out of them
one could create everything
again. Keep it in memory, forever:
the sun, ploughed earth, women,
love, evening, those few words
good for the beginning, keep it all—
perhaps tomorrow we will be
somewhere else, altogether.

Translated from the Polish by Czeslaw Milosz and Robert Hass

EDWARD FIELD
1924 —

Travel by a suburban train may sometimes be an entire odyssey, if we consider the intensity of feelings in the person travelling. Such is the case in this poem by Edward Field. We don't know the reasons for the enormous internal tension in this man; we know only that he experiences a breakthrough in the flowing sequence of joy, fear, and weeping. But the last station means the resolution of his tension, and radiance.

A JOURNEY

When he got up that morning everything was different:
He enjoyed the bright spring day
But he did not realize it exactly, he just enjoyed it.

And walking down the street to the railroad station
Past magnolia trees with dying flowers like old socks
It was a long time since he had breathed so simply.

Tears filled his eyes and it felt good
But he held them back
Because men didn't walk around crying in that town.

Waiting on the platform at the station
The fear came over him of something terrible about to happen:
The train was late and he recited the alphabet to keep hold.

And in its time it came screeching in
And as it went on making its usual stops,
People coming and going, telephone poles passing,

He hid his head behind a newspaper
No longer able to hold back the sobs, and willed his eyes
To follow the rational weavings of the seat fabric.

He didn't do anything violent as he had imagined.
He cried for a long time, but when he finally quieted down
A place in him that had been closed like a fist was open,

And at the end of the ride he stood up and got off that train:
And through the streets and in all the places he lived in later on
He walked, himself at last, a man among men,
With such radiance that everyone looked up and wondered.

CH'IN KUAN
1049—1101

Travel by water is older than other kinds of travel, and sailing has its honorable place in poetry—in China, too, testifying to the importance of rivers and canals in that country.

ALONG THE GRAND CANAL

Hoar frost has congealed
On the deck
Of my little boat.
The water
Is clear and still.
Cold stars beyond counting
Swim alongside.
Thick reeds hide the shore.
You'd think you'd left the earth.
Suddenly there breaks in
Laughter and song.

Translated from the Chinese by Kenneth Rexroth

WANG WEI
701—761

*And here is a charming poem about a marvel of a city to which we arrive by
water for the first time. I, too, lived through a similar experience, in which three
of us, twenty years old, approached the embankment of the city of Constance in
southern Germany by canoe,* A.D. *1931. I should add that if Wang Wei was not a
very willing sailor, he was at least a curious one. He was forced by the duties of
his office to travel, but he longed for a Buddhist detachment, which, in his verse,
is always symbolized by white clouds.*

MORNING, SAILING INTO XINYANG

As my boat sails into Xingze Lake
I am stunned by this glorious city!
A canal meanders by narrow courtyard doors.
Fires and cooking smoke crowd the water.
In these people I see strange customs
and the dialect here is obscure.
In late autumn, fields are abundant.
Morning light. Noise wakes at the city wells.
Fish merchants float on the waves.
Chickens and dogs. Villages on either bank.
I'm heading away from white clouds.
What will become of my solitary sail?

Translated from the Chinese by Tony and Willis Barnstone and Xu Haixin

JOHN HAINES
1924 —

Anybody who has wandered in the mountains will recognize the precision of description in this poem by John Haines.

ON THE MOUNTAIN

We climbed out of timber,
bending on the steep meadow
to look for berries,
then still in the reddening sunlight
went on up the windy shoulder.

A shadow followed us up the mountain
like a black moon rising.
Minute by minute the autumn lamps
on the slope burned out.

Around us the air and the rocks
whispered of night . . .

A great cloud blew from the north,
and the mountain vanished
in the rain and stormlit darkness.

JAAN KAPLINSKI
1941—

*Whoever wants to combine looking and reflection should walk. In this poem a father
and his son walk along a river, in the spring, it seems—which in their country,
Estonia, comes late and has recurrences of frost. The conversation with the son about
the moon is not lacking a curious contradiction: in the Baltic countries, celestial bodies
were once worshipped as divinities, and so one should know how to address the moon.
But, at the same time, the father provides the son with some scientific information.*

WE STARTED HOME, MY SON AND I

We started home, my son and I.
Twilight already. The young moon
stood in the western sky and beside it
a single star. I showed them to my son
and explained how the moon should be greeted
and that this star is the moon's servant.
As we neared home, he said
that the moon is far, as far
as that place where we went.
I told him the moon is much, much farther
and reckoned: if one were to walk
ten kilometers each day, it would take
almost a hundred years to reach the moon.
But this was not what he wanted to hear.
The road was already almost dry.
The river was spread on the marsh; ducks and other waterfowl
crowed the beginning of night. The snow's crust
crackled underfoot—it must
have been freezing again. All the houses' windows
were dark. Only in our kitchen
a light shone. Beside our chimney, the shining moon,
and beside the moon, a single star.

Translated from the Estonian by Jaan Kaplinski with Sam Hamill and Riina Tamm

Places

We visit various places in travelling. Yet travel has always had something mysterious in it, because it is an expectation of the not-yet-known. Perhaps this is a sufficient reason for introducing a separate chapter of poems that deal with places. Yes, we arrive somewhere from our home in another town, city, or village, but not necessarily romanticizing the new, for often we are compelled by circumstances: our employment, our studies, or exile. A given place becomes our temporary home, and yet we preserve a sufficient distance to feel its strangeness, not perceived by those who live there permanently.

WANG CHIEN
736—835

The ancient empire of China was an entire world for its inhabitants. Its remote provinces seemed to be exotic countries distinct by their geography and their people's way of life, such as, for instance, the South, largely identical with the territory of present-day Vietnam.

THE SOUTH

In the southern land many birds sing;
Of towns and cities half are unwalled.
The country markets are thronged by wild tribes;
The mountain-villages bear river-names.
Poisonous mists rise from the damp sands;
Strange fires gleam through the night-rain.
And none passes but the lonely seeker of pearls
Year by year on his way to the South Sea.

Translated from the Chinese by Arthur Waley

TU FU
713—770

A journey to the North of China in autumn, when one could feel in the air the approaching frosts and snows, didn't incline this poet to optimism—who, as we can easily guess, took part in an expedition because of his office.

TRAVELLING NORTHWARD

Screech owls moan in the yellowing
Mulberry trees. Field mice scurry,
Preparing their holes for winter.
Midnight, we cross an old battlefield.
The moonlight shines cold on white bones.

Translated from the Chinese by Kenneth Rexroth

PO CHÜ-I
772—846

The vast network of the state administration employed well-educated men, many of them poets, as was the case for practically all the most eminent literati at the time of the T'ang Dynasty. Disgrace and assignment to a post in a distant province were quite common; thence exile as a topic of poetry. There were also journeys on official missions, escapes from rebellions, service with armies, or just searches for a peaceful retreat in a bucolic setting far from the court and the market. All such situations would give occasion for poems.

AFTER COLLECTING THE AUTUMN TAXES

From these high walls I look at the town below
Where the natives of Pa cluster like a swarm of flies.
How can I govern these people and lead them aright?
I cannot even understand what they say.
But at least I am glad, now that the taxes are in,
To learn that in my province there is no discontent.
I fear its prosperity is not due to me
And was only caused by the year's abundant crops.
The papers I have to deal with are simple and few;
My arbour by the lake is leisurely and still.
In the autumn rain the berries fall from the eaves;
At the evening bell the birds return to the wood.
A broken sunlight quavers over the southern porch
Where I lie on my couch abandoned to idleness.

Translated from the Chinese by Arthur Waley

RAIN

Since I lived a stranger in the City of Hsün-yang
Hour by hour bitter rain has poured.
On few days has the dark sky cleared;
In listless sleep I have spent much time.
The lake has widened till it almost joins the sky;
The clouds sink till they touch the water's face.
Beyond my hedge I hear the boatman's talk;
At the street-end I hear the fisher's song.
Misty birds are lost in yellow air;
Windy sails kick the white waves.
In front of my gate the horse and carriage-way
In a single night has turned into a river-bed.

Translated from the Chinese by Arthur Waley

TU FU
713—770

ANOTHER SPRING

White birds over the grey river.
Scarlet flowers on the green hills.
I watch the Spring go by and wonder
If I shall ever return home.

Translated from the Chinese by Kenneth Rexroth

SU MAN SHU
[dates unknown]

*Sometimes the place of exile was farther than the poet's own continent—here,
within the continent, it was in Japan.*

EXILE IN JAPAN

On the balcony of the tower
I play my flute and watch
The Spring rain.
I wonder
If I ever
Will go home and see
The tide bore
In Chekiang River again.
Straw sandals, an old
Begging bowl, nobody
Knows me. On how many
Bridges have I trampled
The fallen cherry blossoms?

Translated from the Chinese by Kenneth Rexroth

JOSEPH BRODSKY
1940—1996

For a newly arrived immigrant, Russian poet Joseph Brodsky, the American Midwest was a completely exotic land. He introduced young Americans to the arcana of poetry at the University of Michigan in Ann Arbor.

IN THE LAKE DISTRICT

In those days, in a place where dentists thrive
(their daughters order fancy clothes from London;
their painted forceps hold aloft on signboards
a common and abstracted Wisdom Tooth),
there I—whose mouth held ruins more abject
than any Parthenon—a spy, a spearhead
for some fifth column of a rotting culture
(my cover was a lit. professorship),
was living at a college near the most
renowned of the fresh-water lakes; the function
to which I'd been appointed was to wear out
the patience of the ingenuous local youth.

Whatever I wrote then was incomplete:
my lines expired in strings of dots. Collapsing,
I dropped, still fully dressed, upon my bed.
At night I stared up at the darkened ceiling
until I saw a shooting star, which then, conforming to the laws of
    self-combustion,
would flash—before I'd even made a wish—
across my cheek and down onto my pillow.

Translated from the Russian by George L. Kline

LOUIS SIMPSON
1923—

*America, even for an American, may present itself in quite an alien manner, and
the streets of big cities at night seem to contain the essence of alienation, which is
faithfully conveyed by Louis Simpson's poem.*

AFTER MIDNIGHT

The dark streets are deserted,
With only a drugstore glowing
Softly, like a sleeping body;

With one white, naked bulb
In the back, that shines
On suicides and abortions.

Who lives in these dark houses?
I am suddenly aware
I might live here myself.

The garage man returns
And puts the change in my hand,
Counting the singles carefully.

ALLEN GINSBERG
1926—

Fortunately, America is, for the most part, not all big cities—but often little towns and villages. Allen Ginsberg, though a native of New York, lived in his youth in Berkeley and San Francisco, and from that time comes the following poem.

A STRANGE NEW COTTAGE IN BERKELEY

All afternoon cutting bramble blackberries off a tottering
brown fence
   under a low branch with its rotten old apricots miscellaneous
under the leaves,
   fixing the drip in the intricate gut machinery of a new toilet;
   found a good coffee pot in the vines by the porch, rolled a
big tire out of the scarlet bushes, hid my marijuana;
   wet the flowers, playing the sunlit water each to each,
returning for godly extra drops for the stringbeans and daisies;
   three times walked round the grass and sighed absently:
   my reward, when the garden fed me its plums from the
form of a small tree in the corner,
   an angel thoughtful of my stomach, and my dry and love-
lorn tongue.

JAMES APPLEWHITE
1935—

The province and the big metropolis—in America, above all, Babylon: i.e., New
York. But for the inhabitants of the southern states—such as, here, North
Carolina—there is a latent dislike of the Yankees, going back to the Civil War.
James Applewhite, a poet from the South, sends his son on his first trip to Babylon
with a blessing but also with a warning.

PRAYER FOR MY SON

The low river flows like smoked glass.
Small bass guard their nest. Next
To our house, the cardinals in their
Crabapple feed two open mouths.
Parents and offspring, we flex
And swing in this future's coming,
Mirror we look into only darkly.
My youngest is boarding an airplane
To a New York he's never seen.
Raised in such slumberous innocence
Of Bible schools and lemonade,
I adjust poorly to this thirst for
Fame, this electronic buzz prizing
Brilliance and murderers. Oh son,
Know that the psyche has its own
Fame, whether known or not, that
Soul can flame like feathers of a bird.
Grow into your own plumage, brightly,
So that any tree is a marvelous city.
I wave from here by this Indian Eno,
Whose lonely name I make known.

PO CHÜ-I
772—846

There are many varieties of coping with life in exile and Chinese poets are very skillful at them—like this poet, my favorite realist, Po Chü-I. He came up with a good approach to exile.

MADLY SINGING IN THE MOUNTAINS

There is no one among men that has not a special failing;
And my failing consists in writing verses.
I have broken away from the thousand ties of life;
But this infirmity still remains behind.
Each time that I look at a fine landscape,
Each time that I meet a loved friend,
I raise my voice and recite a stanza of poetry
And marvel as though a God had crossed my path.
Ever since the day I was banished to Hsün-yang
Half my time I have lived among the hills.
And often, when I have finished a new poem,
Alone I climb the road to the Eastern Rock.
I lean my body on the banks of white Stone;
I pull down with my hands a green cassia branch.
My mad singing startles the valleys and hills;
The apes and birds all come to peep.
Fearing to become a laughing-stock to the world,
I choose a place that is unfrequented by men.

Translated from the Chinese by Arthur Waley

ELIZABETH BISHOP
1911—1979

Trying to show how poets of various languages and epochs describe things and places, I move among many lives, faces, dresses, each time identifying myself with one character; and I jump in time and geography. It's far from China to Brazil such as it was when it didn't have that name, when the first whites landed on its shores, and a clash occurred between Roman Catholic civilization and Nature, with its demonic and innocent sensuality, and with the people there, "savages," "children of nature." Or perhaps that clash is such as we represent it—we and Elizabeth Bishop, who, besides, lived a long time in Brazil and describes a landscape well known to her.

BRAZIL, JANUARY 1, 1502

. . . embroidered nature . . . tapestried landscape.

—SIR KENNETH CLARK
Landscape into Art

Januaries, Nature greets our eyes
exactly as she must have greeted theirs:
every square inch filling in with foliage—
big leaves, little leaves, and giant leaves,
blue, blue-green, and olive,
with occasional lighter veins and edges,
or a satin underleaf turned over;
monster ferns
in silver-gray relief,
and flowers, too, like giant water lilies
up in the air—up, rather, in the leaves—
purple, yellow, two yellows, pink,
rust red and greenish white;
solid but airy; fresh as if just finished
and taken off the frame.

A blue-white sky, a simple web,
backing for feathery detail:
brief arcs, a pale-green broken wheel,
a few palms, swarthy, squat, but delicate;
and perching there in profile, beaks agape,
the big symbolic birds keep quiet,
each showing only half his puffed and padded,
pure-colored or spotted breast.
Still in the foreground there is Sin:
five sooty dragons near some massy rocks.
The rocks are worked with lichens, gray moonbursts
splattered and overlapping,
threatened from underneath by moss
in lovely hell-green flames,
attacked above
by scaling-ladder vines, oblique and neat,
"one leaf yes and one leaf no"; (in Portuguese).
The lizards scarcely breathe; all eyes
are on the smaller, female one, back-to,
her wicked tail straight up and over,
red as a red-hot wire.

Just so the Christians, hard as nails,
tiny as nails, and glinting,
in creaking armor, came and found it all,
not unfamiliar:
no lovers' walks, no bowers,
no cherries to be picked, no lute music,
but corresponding, nevertheless,
to an old dream of wealth and luxury
already out of style when they left home—
wealth, plus a brand-new pleasure.
Directly after Mass, humming perhaps
L'Homme armé or some such tune,

they ripped away into the hanging fabric,
each out to catch an Indian for himself—
those maddening little women who kept calling,
calling to each other (or had the birds waked up?)
and retreating, always retreating, behind it.

ROLF JACOBSEN
1907—

The goal of European travels, beginning with the Renaissance, was to gain an acquaintance with the marvels of architecture and art left by the past. The privileged place was Italy, and wanderers and pilgrims from Northern Europe would go there. That custom didn't disappear completely, though "cultural tourism" became but a part of the general rush to visit places in the search for new impressions. Rolf Jacobsen, as we see, travelled from his native Norway to Italy not in search of the sun only.

THE CATACOMBS IN SAN CALLISTO

A city in death with the streets caved in and the traffic lights
      still.

A city seen in a broken mirror we have to rub the darkness
      from with our hands.

Beneath the stars and beneath the earth, a city like a laugh
      behind a closed door.

A Venice of night, bridges reflected in dust.

The world's pride, a city with its forehead split and its face
      overgrown with slime.

Thin shreds of roots like fingers and feet, hands and shoulder
      blades of skeletons.

Roots and branches of roots, dead that bend their fingers
      around the dark as around a stone.

A tree up from our broken reality, with its root planted in
      humiliation.

A tree that stretches out over the earth and
      reaches almost to the stars, Arcturus, Capella.

A tree from the earth's heart. Wondrous. Keeping faith.

Translated from the Norwegian by Roger Greenwald

GUNNAR EKËLOF
1907—1968

Another Scandinavian, Swedish poet Gunnar Ekëlof, looked for Greece not among
the vestiges of antiquity but in a pastoral mountain landscape.

GREECE

  O whitewashed chapel
with icons worn out by kisses!
Your door is shut
only with a spike and a twist of wool
such as one gathers among thistles
and twines around the finger
The oil cruse stands ready
and the greasy lamp, and the plate
for him who has a penny
for him who has matches
Old and new icons
a gift of mothers
—occasions have not been wanting—
for him who was left in the pass
for him who was taken as a janissary
for him whose eyesight was emptied
for him who was lost with Markos—
cheap prints under glass
Big as a sheepcote:
Your bells the sheepbells
tinkling somewhere up in the mountains
chapel whose lock is wool.

Translated from the Swedish by Leonard Nathan and James Larson

TOMAS TRANSTRÖMER
1931—

Here, the Greece of islands and ports gives occasion to Swedish poet Tomas Tran-
strömer for a descriptive poem which changes into a moral parable.

SYROS

In Syros' harbor abandoned merchant ships lay idle.
Stem by stem by stem. Moored for many years:
CAPE RION, Monrovia.
KRITOS, Andros.
SCOTIA, Panama.

Dark paintings on the water, they have been hung aside.

Like playthings from our childhood, grown gigantic,
that remind us
of what we never became.

XELATROS, Piraeus.
CASSIOPEIA, Monrovia.
The ocean scans them no more.

But when we first came to Syros, it was at night,
we saw stem by stem by stem in moonlight and thought:
what a powerful fleet, what splendid connections!

Translated from the Swedish by May Swenson and Leif Sjöberg

LINDA GREGG

1942—

Once again Greece, this time seen with the eyes of an American woman, and, to the credit of the poet, we should acknowledge that she was aware of the tragic modern Greece.

NIGHT MUSIC

She sits on the mountain that is her home
and the landscapes slide away. One goes down
and then up to the monastery. One drops away
to a winnowing ring and a farmhouse where a girl
and her mother are hanging the laundry.
There's a tiny port in the distance where
the shore reaches the water. She is numb
and clear because of the grieving in that world.
She thinks of the bandits and soldiers who
return to the places they have destroyed.
Who plant trees and build walls and play music
in the village square evening after evening,
believing the mothers of the boys they killed
and the women they raped will eventually come
out of the white houses in their black dresses
to sit with their children and the old.
Will listen to the music with unreadable eyes.

ADAM ZAGAJEWSKI
1945—

What follows is probably the shortest poem on the twentieth-century mania of visiting places, all over the earth, as tourists.

AUTO MIRROR

In the rear-view mirror suddenly
I saw the bulk of the Beauvais Cathedral;
great things dwell in small ones
for a moment.

Translated from the Polish by Czeslaw Milosz and Robert Hass

SANDOR WEORES
1913—1989

The Hungarian pushta, *a limitless plain, is the subject of this poem by Sandor Weores. This poem surprises me somewhat because Weores was considered a difficult, very avant-garde poet, whereas here he is a painter of the landscape, much in the nineteenth-century tradition.*

THE PLAIN

A muddy-wheeled cart goes lurching
between the poplar trees' wide rows
just where the narrow track
cuts from the main road.

Crops, naked fields, horizon
and sky surround the single horse
and driver in a wide frame,
hiding them in fixity that never alters.

The distant here seems very near
and what's near seems far away:
all sing together as one—
everywhere furrows, lumps of clay—

horse, driver and small cart
rolling the working hours away
through slow centuries,
and buried by the nights and days.

Translated from the Hungarian by J. Kessler

TOMAS TRANSTRÖMER
1931—

A transformation of the landscape, and awareness of the alienation of man in new surroundings, transpire in this poem by Tranströmer.

OUTSKIRTS

Men in overalls the same color as earth rise from a ditch.
It's a transitional place, in stalemate, neither country nor city.
Construction cranes on the horizon want to take the big leap, but
  the clocks are against it.
Concrete piping scattered around laps at the light with cold
  tongues.
Auto-body shops occupy old barns.
Stones throw shadows as sharp as objects on the moon surface.
And these sites keep on getting bigger
like the land bought with Judas' silver: "a potter's field for burying
  strangers."

Translated from the Swedish by Robert Bly

DAVID KIRBY
[date unknown]

A poem on an American student in Paris is a good example of familiarity seasoned with a feeling of not-quite-belonging. Something of the sort may also be found in poems on modern tourism. Neither a short visit nor a longer stay reveals things completely new to the citizen of the global village, yet a certain distance favors observation of the detail.

TO A FRENCH STRUCTURALIST

There's no modesty, Todorov,
in the park where I read:
the young mothers and working girls
raise their skirts and open their blouses
to the sun while the children play,
the old men doze, and I wrestle
with your *Poetics.* When I look again,
perhaps they'll all be naked;
they'll make for the seesaw and jungle gym,
bosoms swinging and long legs flashing
in the midday light. Ah, that clerk
at the Préfecture de Police
looked at me with such disdain
when he asked what I was doing in Paris!
It was a lie, Todorov,
when I shrugged and said, "Nothing."

ANTONIO MACHADO
1895—1939

Willis Barnstone, translator of Wang Wei, considers Antonio Machado to be the most Chinese of Spanish poets and he sees in the following poem an "uncanny closeness" to the Chinese poet he translates.

SUMMER NIGHT

A beautiful summer night.
The tall houses leave
their balcony shutters open
to the wide plaza of the old village.
In the large deserted square,
stone benches, burning bush and acacias
trace their black shadows
symmetrically on the white sand.
In its zenith, the moon; in the tower,
the clock's illuminated globe.
I walk through this ancient village,
alone, like a ghost.

Translated from the Spanish by Willis Barnstone

WANG WEI

701—761

In the nineteenth century people visited certain wonders of nature, for instance, the waterfall of Schaffhausen in Europe, and, in America, Niagara Falls. It seems that in old China, similar wonders also attracted visitors.

A WHITE TURTLE UNDER A WATERFALL

The waterfall on South Mountain hits the rocks,
tosses back its foam with terrifying thunder,
blotting out even face-to-face talk.
Collapsing water and bouncing foam soak blue moss,
old moss so thick
it drowns the spring grass.
Animals are hushed.
Birds fly but don't sing
yet a white turtle plays on the pool's sand floor
        under riotous spray,
sliding about with the torrents.
The people of the land are benevolent.
No angling or net fishing.
The white turtle lives out its life, naturally.

Translated from the Chinese by Tony and Willis Barnstone and Xu Haixin

OU YANG HSIU

1007—1072

There's a considerable number of Chinese poems in this book, for a simple reason: the pictorial qualities of that poetry, expressed in close cooperation with a calligrapher and an artist. "Fisherman" is really like a painting. And in fact the poem has been "translated" into an image by the brush of a painter, many times imitated and often reproduced in books on Chinese art. Drizzle and mist form an obstacle to seeing clearly, and this reminds us that a seeing person—an observer—exists.

FISHERMAN

The wind blows the line out from his fishing pole.
In a straw hat and grass cape the fisherman
Is invisible in the long reeds.
In the fine spring rain it is impossible to see very far
And the mist rising from the water has hidden the hills.

Translated from the Chinese by Kenneth Rexroth

LIU TSUNG-YÜAN
773—819

A fisherman in the landscape was a beloved subject of poets and painters. This poem, however, seems to me quite complicated, in spite of its apparent simplicity. For here there is action, and the fisherman himself appears only toward the end, as somebody who rows somewhere far.

OLD FISHERMAN

Old fisherman spends his night beneath the western cliffs.
At dawn, he boils Hsiang's waters, burns bamboo of Ch'u.
When the mist's burned off, and the sun's come out, he's gone.
The slap of the oars: the mountain waters green.
Turn and look, at heaven's edge, he's moving with the flow.
Above the cliffs the aimless clouds go too.

Translated from the Chinese by J. P. Seaton

WANG WEI
701—761

And now a short, economic (in movements of word and brush) poem by Wang Wei.

MAGNOLIA BASIN

On branch tips the hibiscus bloom.
The mountains show off red calices.
Nobody. A silent cottage in the valley.
One by one flowers open, then fall.

Translated from the Chinese by Tony and Willis Barnstone and Xu Haixin

The Moment

Poetry feeds on the remembrance of our perceptions that are no more, since they belong to a moment in the past. That past may be of a year or of a minute; we do not write of what is presently happening, but always of something at a remove, albeit even the shortest. Remembrance of the things that are past allows for a dispassionate description: "Distance is the soul of beauty" (Simone Weil).

A moment is like a frame of film. Some poems attempt to catch and fix a moment, and thus to stop the film of time, to glance attentively at one of its frames. Probably modern poetry has been influenced by film in this respect. After all, a frame is a unit of space-time; i.e., a moment is not an abstraction, but is filled with what is seen by the eye. Time is not "an element" stretching infinitely, in a linear way, backwards and forwards; it always offers itself to the eye as saturated with a fragment of space, as in a film frame. This has been expressed in a famous passage of St. Augustine's *Confessions*: "So what is time? If no one asks me, I know: if I want to explain it to a person who asks, I do not know anymore and yet I affirm with certainty that, had nothing passed, there would not be past time—had nothing happened there would not be future time, had nothing existed, there would not be present time."

Some poems describe a moment placed far back in time; some create an illusion of the present—for instance, Walt Whitman's short poems, scenes of the Civil War, that resemble illustrations drawn for a magazine. When one approaches a poem it is interesting to ask where—how far away in time—a described moment resides. It makes a reader more attentive—and reading a poem is, after all, always an exercise in attention.

WALT WHITMAN
1819—1892

CAVALRY CROSSING A FORD

A line in long array where they wind betwixt green islands,
They take a serpentine course, their arms flash in the sun—
    hark to the musical clank,
Behold the silvery river, in it the splashing horses loitering
    stop to drink,
Behold the brown-faced men, each group, each person a
    picture, the negligent rest on the saddles,
Some emerge on the opposite bank, others are just entering
    the ford—while,
Scarlet and blue and snowy white,
The guidon flags flutter gayly in the wind.

ALOYSIUS BERTRAND
1807—1841

This poem in prose by French poet Aloysius Bertrand is somewhat similar to a painting. It describes what a mason, Knupfer, sees while standing high on a scaffolding above a city. Yet there are, here, two moments, and between them, duration, because Knupfer, after his day's work, notices something else in the evening—the fire in a village situated not far from the city. This is a fine poem, but a bit too literary. It looks as if the author, influenced by his reading, decided to give a synthetic drawing of a city with a cathedral in the middle.

THE MASON

The Master Mason. —Look at these bastions, these buttresses; one would say they were built for eternity.

SCHILLER,
William Tell

The mason Abraham Knupfer is singing, trowel in hand, scaffolded so high in the air that, reading the Gothic verses on the great bell, he puts his feet on a level with both the church with thirty buttresses and the town with thirty churches.

He sees the stone monsters vomit the water from the slates into the confused abyss of galleries, windows, pendentives, bell-towers, turrets, roofs, and timber work, which the slanting motionless wing of the falcon marks with a grey spot.

He sees the fortifications outlined in a star, the citadel cocking itself up like a hen in a pie, the palace courtyards where the sun dries up the fountains and the monastery cloisters where the shadow turns around the pillars.

The imperial troops are quartered in the suburb. There is a horseman beating a drum down there. Abraham Knupfer makes out his tricorn hat, his shoulder-knots of red wool, his cockade crossed with a gimp, and his pigtail knotted with a ribbon.

He sees more: there are old soldiers who, in the park adorned with huge leafy branches, on broad emerald lawns, riddle with arquebus shots a wooden bird fixed to the top of a maypole.

And in the evening, when the melodious nave of the cathedral went to sleep lying with its arms in a cross, he saw from his ladder on the horizon, a village, set on fire by soldiers, flaming like a comet in the blue sky.

Translated from the French by E. D. Hartley

KENNETH REXROTH
1905—1982

To sojourn in the now. Kenneth Rexroth, whom I knew personally, was a kind
of father of the Beat movement in poetry, which was born in San Francisco and
Berkeley. At that time Rexroth was already considered the most eminent poet in
California, in those circles which took an interest in poetry. Sympathetic toward
the young, and close to them in his anarchist convictions, he backed the doings of
disheveled and savage youngsters who, however, were better educated than one might
guess from their subversive syntax. An excellent translator of Chinese and Japanese
poets; cosmopolitan, because he passed some time in France (he published a volume
of Oscar Milosz's poems in his translation) and in Japan; he entered into the spirit
of Buddhism, of which some of his poems remind us, resembling the poetry of Asia.
Of course he was also a reader of Christian mystics, such as Jacob Boehme, a
German cobbler of the seventeenth century, author of spiritual works.

SIGNATURE OF ALL THINGS
Part I

My head and shoulders, and my book
In the cool shade, and my body
Stretched bathing in the sun, I lie
Reading beside the waterfall—
Boehme's "Signature of All Things."
Through the deep July day the leaves
Of the laurel, all the colors
Of gold, spin down through the moving
Deep laurel shade all day. They float
On the mirrored sky and forest
For a while, and then, still slowly
Spinning, sink through the crystal deep
Of the pool to its leaf gold floor.
The saint saw the world as streaming
In the electrolysis of love.
I put him by and gaze through shade

Folded into shade of slender
Laurel trunks and leaves filled with sun.
The wren broods in her moss domed nest.
A newt struggles with a white moth
Drowning in the pool. The hawks scream,
Playing together on the ceiling
Of heaven. The long hours go by.
I think of those who have loved me,
Of all the mountains I have climbed,
Of all the seas I have swum in.
The evil of the world sinks.
My own sin and trouble fall away
Like Christian's bundle, and I watch
My forty summers fall like falling
Leaves and falling water held
Eternally in summer air.

Another poem of Rexroth's is a description of what happened to him on a certain summer night, yet in order to render the experience in all its intensity he has to speak of it in the present tense. Let us imagine the effect were we to introduce the past tense. "I took a telescope, I looked, my eyes and brain were not asleep, I didn't know where I began or ended." Instead of immediate experience, we would introduce remembrance, whereas in the poem perception is given directly.

THE HEART OF HERAKLES

Lying under the stars,
In the summer night,
Late, while the autumn
Constellations climb the sky,
As the Cluster of Hercules
Falls down the west
I put the telescope by
And watch Deneb
Move towards the zenith.
My body is asleep. Only
My eyes and brain are awake.
The stars stand around me
Like gold eyes. I can no longer
Tell where I begin and leave off.
The faint breeze in the dark pines,
And the invisible grass,
The tipping earth, swarming stars
Have an eye that sees itself.

TU FU
713—770

Rexroth translated much Tu Fu, the leading poet of the T'ung Dynasty. As far as I know, he was helped by French translations. Nevertheless, comparing his versions with others, I admire his conciseness and choices of image. In "Sunset" Tu Fu enumerates actions of nature and of people at dusk-time (a series of moments). Mention of the "thousand cares" at the end of the poem introduces duration, and thus the poem, though it praises the very capturing of a moment, also expresses joy at the wine's ability to liberate us from the burden of the past.

SUNSET

Sunset glitters on the beads
Of the curtains. Spring flowers
Bloom in the valley. The gardens
Along the river are filled
With perfume. Smoke of cooking
Fires drifts over the slow barges.
Sparrows hop and tumble in
The branches. Whirling insects
Swarm in the air. Who discovered
That one cup of thick wine
Will dispel a thousand cares?

Translated from the Chinese by Kenneth Rexroth

What attracts me to the Chinese poets most is their ability to draw with a few dashes a certain situation, for instance, in this poem by Tu Fu, the hour before dawn, after an entire night of carousing with friends.

WINTER DAWN

The men and beasts of the zodiac
Have marched over us once more.
Green wine bottles and red lobster shells,
Both emptied, litter the table.
"Should auld acquaintance be forgot?" Each
Sits listening to his own thoughts,
And the sound of cars starting outside.
The birds in the eaves are restless,
Because of the noise and light. Soon now
In the winter dawn I will face
My fortieth year. Borne headlong
Towards the long shadows of sunset
By the headstrong, stubborn moments,
Life whirls past like drunken wildfire.

Translated from the Chinese by Kenneth Rexroth

Is this Tu Fu poem also about a moment? It enumerates the most common features of springtime, so perhaps this is just a poem about that season. But a man who writes clearly places himself in the now, *and the word "now" could really precede every sentence.*

SOUTH WIND

The days grow long, the mountains
Beautiful. The south wind blows
Over blossoming meadows.
Newly arrived swallows dart
Over the streaming marshes.
Ducks in pairs drowse on the warm sand.

Translated from the Chinese by Kenneth Rexroth

One more by Tu Fu: the moment immediately after rain. "Ten thousand miles"
means simply a great distance, and not a precise measure. "West wind" simply
blows from far away, over the continent.

CLEAR AFTER RAIN

Autumn, cloud blades on the horizon.
The west wind blows from ten thousand miles.
Dawn, in the clear morning air,
Farmers busy after long rain.
The desert trees shed their few green leaves.
The mountain pears are tiny but ripe.
A Tartar flute plays by the city gate.
A single wild goose climbs into the void.

Translated from the Chinese by Kenneth Rexroth

GARY SNYDER
1930—

This poem by Gary Snyder is like noting down what, precisely, happens; in other words, the time between seeing and noting is very short. The snowpeak changes color, shadows gather in the gorge, as if the writer sitting by the fire had an open notebook and tried to fix what he saw and what he, himself, was doing. Of course, the poem might not have been written at that moment in that landscape, but, rather, uses this device.

LATE OCTOBER CAMPING IN THE SAWTOOTHS

Sunlight climbs the snowpeak
    glowing pale red
Cold sinks into the gorge
    shadows merge.
Building a fire of pine twigs
    at the foot of a cliff,
Drinking hot tea from a tin cup
    in the chill air—
Pull on a sweater and roll a smoke.
    a leaf
    beyond fire
Sparkles with nightfall frost.

KEITH WILSON
1927—

In this poem by Keith Wilson the description of the twilight is, again, in the
present tense. There is a defined place from which the observer looks at the changes
in the falling night. He stands in the yard and watches the walls and windows of
his house. He notices a candle in his daughter's hand, her lit face; he hears pecans
falling from the tree, which means that the tree rises above the roof of the house;
he is aware of the moon rising and of its light, like platinum. And so there is a
convention of simultaneity between observation and recording.

DUSK IN MY BACKYARD
San Miguel, N.M.

The long black night
moves over my walls:
inside a candle is lighted
by one of my daughters.

Even from here I can see
the illuminated eyes, bright
face of the child before flame.

It's nearly time to go in.
The wind is cooler now,
pecans drop, rattle down—

the tin roof of our house
rivers to platinum in the early moon.
Dogs bark & in the house, wine, laughter.

TED KOOSER
1939—

This poem, on a little town in Minnesota, is a synthetic image or even a collage. There is no single observer. First, we see the last car of a moving train, then we receive information about two lights in the darkness, one a bulb in the prison, the other a flashlight handled by an old woman going downstairs to the bathroom. And so altogether a province. The prison is an important building; an old house with cats belongs to a lone woman (the husband dead, children somewhere far away). Simultaneous images—moments are recaptured.

LATE LIGHTS IN MINNESOTA

At the end of a freight train rolling away,
a hand swinging a lantern.
The only lights left behind in the town
are a bulb burning cold in the jail,
and high in one house,
a five-battery flashlight
pulling an old woman downstairs to the toilet
among the red eyes of her cats.

TOMAS TRANSTRÖMER
1931—

This poem by Tranströmer is the most literally spoken in the now, and it's so impressive that we forget to ask when—how long ago—the observer lived through it. It's like a snapshot, though enriched by things known from the past, in a dream or during illness.

TRACKS

Night, two o'clock: moonlight. The train has stopped
in the middle of the plain. Distant bright points of a town
twinkle cold on the horizon.

As when someone has gone into a dream so far
that he'll never remember he was there
when he comes back to his room.

And as when someone goes into a sickness so deep
that all his former days become twinkling points, a swarm,
cold and feeble on the horizon.

The train stands perfectly still.
Two o'clock: full moonlight, few stars.

Translated from the Swedish by Robert Bly

ROLF JACOBSEN
1907—

This poem by an eminent Norwegian poet, Rolf Jacobsen, notes down a moment at dawn and concentrates attention on the traces left by tires, then changes its perspective to that of an ant inside the letter "G," which for an ant is a tremendous obstacle.

RUBBER

One pale morning in June at four o'clock
when the country roads were still gray and wet
in their endless tunnels of forest,
a car had passed over the clay
just where the ant came out busily with its pine needle now
and kept wandering around in the big G of "Goodyear"
that was imprinted in the sand of country roads
for a hundred and twenty kilometers.
Pine needles are heavy.
Time after time it slid back down with its tottering load
and worked its way up again
and slipped back again.
Outward bound across the great, cloud-illuminated Sahara.

Translated from the Norwegian by Roger Greenwald

AL ZOLYNAS
1945—

In the life of California poet Al Zolynas, a moment of activity, namely, washing dishes, and the moment of the poem itself are not separated, and we can even imagine that he talks to himself washing dishes and that a tape has recorded his words. This would be a new kind of coping with time, though we know that composition is an integral part of poetry, and that direct reaction to events is rather rare. We are rather inclined to consider this poem a composition on the subject of washing dishes, with a consciously maintained illusion of the present tense.

ZEN OF HOUSEWORK

I look over my own shoulder
down my arms
to where they disappear under water
into hands inside pink rubber gloves
moiling among dinner dishes.

My hands lift a wine glass,
holding it by the stem and under the bowl.
It breaks the surface
like a chalice
rising from a medieval lake.

Full of the grey wine
of domesticity, the glass floats
to the level of my eyes.
Behind it, through the window
above the sink, the sun, among
a ceremony of sparrows and bare branches
is setting in Western America.

I can see thousands of droplets
of steam—each a tiny spectrum—rising
from my goblet of grey wine.

They sway, changing directions
constantly—like a school of playful fish,
or like the sheer curtain
on the window to another world.

Ah, grey sacrament of the mundane!

BRONISLAW MAJ
1953—

This poem by Bronislaw Maj tells about a moment lived long ago, when he was
four. The intensity of perception was so great that it remains fixed in memory as
forever present, as if it had just taken place. He uses the present tense, and perhaps
for the best, because the past tense might be somewhat sentimental.

AN AUGUST AFTERNOON

An August afternoon. Even here is heard
the rush of the glittering Raba.
We look at the mountains,
my mother and I. How clear the air is:
every dark spruce on Mount Lubon
is seen distinctly as if it grew in our garden.
An astonishing phenomenon—it astonishes my mother
and me. I am four and do not know
what it means *to be four.* I am
happy: I do not know what *to be* means
or *happiness.* I know my mother
sees and feels what I do. And I know
that as always in the evening
we will take a walk
far, up to the woods, already before
long.

Translated from the Polish by Czeslaw Milosz and Robert Hass

RAYMOND CARVER
1938—1988

Just before daybreak, when it is still dark, an electrical blackout causes the speaker to look outside at the landscape, which appears extraordinarily calm. The speaker feels pure inside at that moment. Later the same morning, electricity is restored and "things stood as they had before."

THE WINDOW

A storm blew in last night and knocked out
the electricity. When I looked
through the window, the trees were translucent.
Bent and covered with rime. A vast calm
lay over the countryside.
I knew better. But at that moment
I felt I'd never in my life made any
false promises, nor committed
so much as one indecent act. My thoughts
were virtuous. Later on that morning,
of course, electricity was restored.
The sun moved from behind the clouds,
melting the hoarfrost.
And things stood as they had before.

JEAN FOLLAIN
1903—1971

An opposition between once in the past and now, in this poem by French poet Jean Follain, begins with a thought about a woman who buys an elixir in a city hundreds or thousands of years ago. The word "elixir" is important because it has magical connotations. What if she were buying cabbage? We don't know anything about this woman; we receive no image of her, and yet our awareness that she lived, existed, liberates in us a feeling of closeness to her, in her flesh. A woman who died long ago becomes like our contemporary women. The poem conveys a very complex set of feelings about the frailty and transience of the body, which is precisely what makes our life "vertiginous."

BUYING

She was buying an elixir
in a city
of bygone times
yet we should think of her
now when shoulders are as white
and wrists as fine
flesh as sweet
Oh, vertiginous life!

Translated from the French by Heather McHugh

I have doubts about some of Follain's poems. Since my ideal is simplicity, a work that pushes conciseness beyond a certain limit seems to me too literary, or too sophisticated, which are often equated. "Black Meat" expects the reader to guess that primitive cave dwellers are involved, for whom precious stones would have no value, and we don't know why those stones are there, where hunters used to carve their game.

BLACK MEAT

Around stones called precious
which only their own
dust can wear down
the eaters of venison
carve in silence
their black meat
the trees on the horizon
imitate in outline
a giant sentence.

Translated from the French by W. S. Merwin

Frankly, the modernist technique consisting of unexpected associations is not to my liking, as at the end of this poem, in which drops of blood fall upon a road. In order to understand this, we must presume that there are hunters in the neighborhood, that they shot a bird, and that a wounded bird flies over the road.

SCHOOL AND NATURE

Drawn on the blackboard
in the classroom in a town
a circle remained intact
and the teacher's chair was deserted
and the students had gone
one sailing on the flood
another plowing alone
and the road went winding
a bird letting fall
the dark drops of its blood.

Translated from the French by W. S. Merwin

LINDA GREGG
1942—

*This poem of Linda Gregg's is maintained entirely in the convention of narrating
in the now. The narrator, as we guess, sits before a house in a Greek town and
what she sees and hears makes the content of the poem. And thus we are close to
the technique of communicating immediately one's perceptions. Yet even if one can
command: "Oh, Moment, stop, you are beautiful," it is not a landscape completely
free from anxiety. "The dark thing," the sea seen through the leaves, acquires in
one's consciousness the symbolical meaning of danger, and in that manner "now"
is entangled in the past and the future.*

A DARK THING INSIDE THE DAY

So many want to be lifted by song and dancing,
and this morning it is easy to understand.
I write in the sound of chirping birds hidden
in the almond trees, the almonds still green
and thriving in the foliage. Up the street,
a man is hammering to make a new house as doves
continue their cooing forever. Bees humming
and high above that a brilliant clear sky.
The roses are blooming and I smell the sweetness.
Everything desirable is here already in abundance.
And the sea. The dark thing is hardly visible
in the leaves, under the sheen. We sleep easily.
So I bring no sad stories to warn the heart.
All the flowers are adult this year. The good
world gives and the white doves praise all of it.

ALEKSANDER WAT
1900–1967

This poem by Aleksander Wat is interesting for me because I know the place from
which he looks down on the landscape of Provence. And that is La Messuguière,
the retreat for writers, near Cabris. "How hot it is." This reminder is here to
create the impression that this scenery is observed at that particular moment. The
description of what one sees from above is precise, the comparisons—hand as wing,
women as olives, little church as cypress and shepherd—introduce reflection, as
does the mention of the youth of the world. The conclusion is unexpected. The
landscape is dramatized by the personal situation of the onlooker, as he realizes his
situation in a life of exile, far from the country where he was born, Poland.

FROM "SONGS OF A WANDERER"

It is the nature of the highest objective art to be clean.
The Muses are maidens.

A. LANG
Homer and Anthropology

So beautiful the lungs
are breathless. The hand remembers:
I was a wing.
Blue. The peaks in ruddy
gold. Women of that land—
small olives. On a spacious saucer
wisps of smoke, houses, pastures, roads.
Interlacing of roads, o holy diligence
of man. How hot it is! The miracle
of shade returns. A shepherd, sheep, a dog, a ram
all in gilded bells. Olive trees
in twisted benevolence. A cypress—their lone shepherd. A village
on a Cabris cliff, protected
by its tiled roofs. And a church its cypress and shepherd.
Young day, young times, young world.

Birds listen, intently silent. Only a rooster crowing
from below in the hamlet of Spéracèdes. How
hot it is. It's bitter to die on foreign soil.
It's sweet to live in France.

Translated from the Polish by Czeslaw Milosz and Leonard Nathan

OSCAR V. DE L. MILOSZ
1877—1939

This French poet of Lithuanian origin, Oscar V. de L. Milosz, my relative, has found fine translators in English, beginning with Ezra Pound, and followed by Kenneth Rexroth, David Gascoyne. His poetry is steeped in the aura of the epoch of symbolism.

THE BRIDGE

Dead leaves are falling in the dormant air.
Look, my dear, what autumn did to our dear isle!
How pale it is!
What an orphan it is, so humble and docile!
Bells ring and ring at Saint-Louis-en-Isle
For a dead fuchsia of the bargemaster's wife.
Heads low, two horses, obedient, sleepy, take their last bath.
A big black dog barks and threatens from afar.
On the bridge only I and my child:
Her faded dress, frail shoulders, face white,
Flowers in her hands.
Oh my child! What will the coming time bring!
To them! To us! Oh my child! What will the coming time bring!

Translated from the French by Czeslaw Milosz and Robert Hass

JAAN KAPLINSKI
1941—

This is a perfect remembrance of things past. The narrator knows his botany well.
He is able to name, in Latin, some ordinary plants beneath his feet, and one of
those plants, Potentilla Anserina, *goose tansy, suddenly opens the memory of*
childhood.

MY WIFE AND CHILDREN

My wife and children were waiting for ice cream.
For a while, I had nothing else to do
but stand, looking underfoot:
Festuca, Poa, Trifolium repens, Taraxacum vulgare
and just on the edge of the sidewalk, where people
often pass hurrying from the market hall to the bus station,
it's you, Potentilla Anserina, an old acquaintance
from Tartumaa and Võrumaa farmyards
we can never forget as we cannot also forget
gooseshit I so often stepped in
and that stuck between my toes.

Translated from the Estonian by Jaan Kaplinski with Sam Hamill and Riina Tamm

WALT WHITMAN
1819—1892

A moment and remembrance, this time in Walt Whitman, though here only a campfire and darkness with army tents are concrete, while the subject of the narrator's thoughts is "solemn and sweet and slow."

BY THE BIVOUAC'S FITFUL FLAME

By the bivouac's fitful flame,
A procession winding around me, solemn and sweet and
slow—but first I note,
The tents of the sleeping army, the fields' and woods' dim outline,
The darkness lit by spots of kindled fire, the silence,
Like a phantom far or near an occasional figure moving,
The shrubs and trees, (as I lift my eyes they seem to be
stealthily watching me,)
While wind in procession thoughts, O tender and wondrous
   thoughts,
Of life and death, of home and the past and loved, and of
those that are far away;
A solemn and slow procession there as I sit on the ground,
By the bivouac's fitful flame.

EAMON GRENNAN

1941—

Human windows and everything that occurs behind them. The curiosity of a passerby,
but also a voyeur, or a poet, a fairy-tale teller, a novelist, composing all biography
and tales from a detail seen through a window. It may last just an instant, but
sometimes, as in this poem by an Irish poet, probably a little longer.

WOMAN AT LIT WINDOW

Perhaps if she stood for an hour like that
and I could stand to stand in the dark
just looking, I might get it right, every
fine line in place: the veins of the hand
reaching up to the blind-cord, etch
of the neck in profile, the white
and violet shell of the ear
in its whorl of light, that neatly
circled strain against a black
cotton sweater. For a few seconds

she is staring through me
where I stand wondering what I'll do
if she starts
on that stage of light
taking her clothes off. But she only
frowns out at nothing or herself
in the glass, and I think I could,
if we stood for an hour like this,
get some of the real details down. But
already, even as she lowers the blind,
she's turning away, leaving a blank
ivory square of brightness
to float alone in the dark, the faint
grey outline of the house
around it. Newly risen, the half moon casts

my shadow on the path
skinned with grainy radiance
as I make my way back
to my own place
among the trees, a host of fireflies
in fragrant silence and native ease
pricking the dark around me
with their pulse of light.

CHARLES SIMIC
1938—

A dream may transform a moment lived once, at one time, and change it into part of a nightmare. Charles Simic, an American poet born in Serbia, remembers the time of the German occupation in his country. This scene from childhood is put in relief as the present which is no more, but which now, when the poet writes, constantly returns in dreams. In other words, it has its own present, of a new kind, on the first page of a diary of dreams.

EMPIRE OF DREAMS

On the first page of my dreambook
It's always evening
In an occupied country.
Hour before the curfew.
A small provincial city.
The houses all dark.
The store-fronts gutted.

I am on a street corner
Where I shouldn't be.
Alone and coatless
I have gone out to look
For a black dog who answers to my whistle.
I have a kind of halloween mask
Which I am afraid to put on.

PO CHÜ-I
772—846

And here a true study of the moment, and of the relationship between dreams and
reality, by Po Chü-I.

SLEEPING ON HORSEBACK

We had ridden long and were still far from the inn;
My eyes grew dim; for a moment I fell asleep.
Under my right arm the whip still dangled;
In my left hand the reins for an instant slackened.
Suddenly I woke and turned to question my groom.
"We have gone a hundred paces since you fell asleep."
Body and spirit for a while had changed place;
Swift and slow had turned to their contraries.
For these few steps that my horse had carried me
Had taken in my dream countless aeons of time!
True indeed is that saying of Wise Men
"A hundred years are but a moment of sleep."

Translated from the Chinese by Arthur Waley

WAYNE DODD
1930—

Rain doesn't appear often in poetry but it has its right of citizenship, and usually induces a mood because certain states of withdrawal and meditation are associated with rain.

OF RAIN AND AIR

All day I have been closed up
inside rooms, speaking of trivial
matters. Now at last I have come out
into the night, myself a center

of darkness.
Beneath the clouds the low sky glows
with scattered light. I can hardly think
this is happening. Here in this bright absence

of day, I feel myself opening out
with contentment.
All around me the soft rain is whispering
of thousands of feet of air

invisible above us.

SANDOR WEORES
1913—1989

*This poem by a Hungarian, Sandor Weores, builds upon the symbolic value of
rain, which, after all, is water, abundance, a giver of the green, of growth, of
crops. In Weores, the desire to become rain is his longing for the descent of grace
into human life. For rain is also often the symbol of grace falling from above, a
magnanimous gift, of liquid penetration, and the poem praises liberation from in-
hibitions that hamper our love for the human tribe.*

RAIN

The rain's pounding away
    at the rusty eaves.
Twirling, sliding bubbling foam—
    well, that's rain.

You too, and I should walk now
    as free as that
on cloud, on air, the meadow
    and the vapor roads.

Move around up there and here below
    like this liquid thing,
flowing into human life on rooftops
    and on shoes.

Translated from the Hungarian by J. Kessler

People Among People

People observe and describe people, people pronounce their opinions on people, but, above all else, people are bound to people by feelings of love, hate, compassion, fear, admiration, loathing. It is not certain whether good poetry can arise from hatred. My anthology shows that I select mostly poems that express warm feelings. At the risk of being pedantic, it is worthwhile to invoke here three Greek words denoting kinds of love. *Eros* is sexual love, but not only such, because it is "an intermediary between gods and humans," an unlimited desire, a true motoric force of creativity in art and science. *Agape* is love of our fellow men, love-empathy, allowing us to see in another human being a creature as frail and as easily hurt as we are ourselves: that is the same as Latin *caritas*, charity. A third Greek word, *storge,* denotes a tender care, affection uniting parents and children. Perhaps some teachers feel such a love for their pupils. It is also not impossible that *storge* may be applied to the relationship between a poet and generations of readers to come: underneath the ambition to perfect one's art without hope of being rewarded by contemporaries lurks a magnanimity of gift-offering to posterity.

WANG WEI

701—761

I will begin with a poem of observation, which would be less interesting had our contemporaries been involved. But if we think about these characters, that they lived some twelve hundred years ago, then their faults and sins, so arch-human, incline us to indulgence and even sympathy.

SONG ABOUT XI SHI

Her beauty casts a spell on everyone.
How could Xi Shi stay poor so long?
In the morning she was washing clothes in the Yue
    River,
In the evening she was a concubine in the palace
    of Wu.
When she was poor, was she out of the ordinary?
Now rich, she is rare.
Her attendants apply her powders and rouge,
others dress her in silks.
The king favors her and it fans her arrogance.
She can do no wrong.
Of her old friends who washed silks with her,
none share her carriage.
In her village her best friend is ugly. It's hopeless
to imitate Lady Xi Shi's cunning frowns.

Translated from the Chinese by Tony and Willis Barnstone and Xu Haixin

The next poem is an observation-portrait, and the poor scholar who appears here is familiar; he may even provoke warm feelings in his successors, struggling against poverty in societies addicted to the cult of money.

DANCING WOMAN, COCKFIGHTER HUSBAND, AND THE IMPOVERISHED SAGE

The woman from Zhao sings dirty songs
and does dances of Handan
while her husband knocks about, puts on cockfights
for the king of Qi.
With yellow gold he buys songs and laughter from
    a whore.
He never counts his coins.

Xu and Shi, relatives of the Emperor, often come
    to his house.
Their high gates are crowded with four-horse carriages.
A scholar lives in their guest house,
bragging about his rich patron, Zou Lu.
For thirty years his meals are the books he eagerly
    consumes
but his waist belt has no money in it.
His is the way of scholars, of the sage.
All his life he is poor.

Translated from the Chinese by Tony and Willis Barnstone and Xu Haixin

TU FU
713—770

Tu Fu is probably the biggest name in old Chinese poetry. His complaint about the lack of recognition in his lifetime brings to mind the fate of eminent artists of the nineteenth and twentieth centuries, who acquired fame only after their deaths; had they obtained but a small fraction from the sale of their books and paintings, it would have been very useful to them. Reading this poem I reflect upon the obstinacy of artists. Whence comes our passion, our zeal, in working at the risk of possible loss? Is this only ambition, or a bond with people who might come after us, some kind of love?

TO PI SSU YAO

We have talent. People call us
The leading poets of our day.
Too bad, our homes are humble,
Our recognition trivial.
Hungry, ill clothed, servants treat
Us with contempt. In the prime
Of life, our faces are wrinkled.
Who cares about either of us,
Or our troubles? We are our own
Audience. We appreciate
Each other's literary
Merits. Our poems will be handed
Down along with great dead poets'.
We can console each other.
At least we shall have descendants.

Translated from the Chinese by Kenneth Rexroth

MEI YAO CH'EN
1002—1060

Now a true love poem about the love of man and woman, husband and wife, but,
above all, about mutual tenderness.

A DREAM AT NIGHT

In broad daylight I dream I
Am with her. At night I dream
She is still at my side. She
Carries her kit of colored
Threads. I see her image bent
Over her bag of silks. She
Mends and alters my clothes and
Worries for fear I might look
Worn and ragged. Dead, she watches
Over my life. Her constant
Memory draws me towards death.

Translated from the Chinese by Kenneth Rexroth

SEAMUS HEANEY
1939—

All poetry of Seamus Heaney is rooted in his native Ireland, in his country childhood, country labors, and Catholic rites. This reticent and modestly entitled poem is in Fact, as biographers of the poet know, a farewell to his mother.

FROM "CLEARANCES," IN MEMORIAM M.K.H. (1911–1984)

When all the others were away at Mass
I was all hers as we peeled potatoes.
They broke the silence, let fall one by one
Like solder weeping off the soldering iron:
Cold comforts set between us, things to share
Gleaming in a bucket of clean water.
And again let fall. Little pleasant splashes
From each other's work would bring us to our senses.

So while the parish priest at her bedside
Went hammer and tongs at the prayers for the dying
And some were responding and some crying
I remembered her head bent towards my head,
Her breath in mine, our fluent dipping knives—
Never closer the whole rest of our lives.

CONSTANTINE CAVAFY
1863—1933

Cavafy has written one short poem about a mother's love. As usual in his work, he takes Greece as a background, its islands, its sailors, and its religion, here Christian in its Orthodox variety.

SUPPLICATION

The sea took a sailor to its deep. —
His mother, unsuspecting, goes to light

a tall candle before the Virgin Mary
for his speedy return and for fine weather —

and always she cocks her ear to windward.
But while she prays and implores,

the icon listens, solemn and sad, knowing well
that the son she expects will no longer return.

Translated from the Greek by Rae Dalven

Walt Whitman had avid eyes. He wanted to see everything, to memorize everything, and to enclose it all in his poems. But he remains for us primarily a poet of great heart, of all-embracing love, which fuses its varieties into one love, erotic, but also compassionate, protective, and marvelling at everything great and magnificent in man. This aspect of his poetry prompted me to place several fragments of his oeuvre in this chapter.

FROM "I SING THE BODY ELECTRIC"

I knew a man, a common farmer, the father of five sons,
And in them the fathers of sons, and in them the fathers of sons.

This man was of wonderful vigor, calmness, beauty of person,
The shape of his head, the pale yellow and white of his hair and
    beard, the immeasurable meaning of his black eyes, the
    richness and breadth of his manners.
These I used to go and visit him to see, he was wise also,
He was six feet tall, he was over eighty years old, his sons were
    massive, clean, bearded, tan-faced, handsome,
They and his daughters loved him, all who saw him loved him,
They did not love him by allowance, they loved him with personal
    love,
He drank water only, the blood show'd like scarlet through the
    clear-brown skin of his face,
He was a frequent gunner and fisher, he sail'd his boat himself,
    he had a fine one presented to him by a ship-joiner,
    he had fowling-pieces presented to him by men that loved him,
When he went with his five sons and many grand-sons to hunt or
    fish, you would pick him out as the most beautiful and
    vigorous of the gang,
You would wish long and long to be with him, you would wish to
    sit by him in the boat that you and he might touch each
    other.

Some Civil War poems of Whitman's should be placed here, because they are the
most direct in invoking the dead of that war.

AS TOILSOME I WANDER'D VIRGINIA'S WOODS

As toilsome I wander'd Virginia's woods,
To the music of rustling leaves kick'd by my feet, (for
    'twas autumn,)
I mark'd at the foot of a tree the grave of a soldier;
Mortally wounded he and buried on the retreat, (easily all
    could I understand,)
The halt of a mid-day hour, when up! no time to lose—yet
    this sign left,
On a tablet scrawl'd and nail'd on the tree by the grave,
Bold, cautious, true, and my loving comrade.

Long, long I muse, then on my way go wandering,
Many a changeful season to follow, and many a scene of life,
Yet at times through changeful season and scene, abrupt, alone,
    or in the crowded street,
Comes before me the unknown soldier's grave, comes the
    inscription rude in Virginia's woods,
Bold, cautious, true, and my loving comrade.

A SIGHT IN CAMP IN THE DAYBREAK
GRAY AND DIM

A sight in camp in the daybreak gray and dim,
As from my tent I emerge so early sleepless,
As slow I walk in the cool fresh air the path near by the
    hospital tent,
Three forms I see on stretchers lying, brought out there
    untended lying,
Over each the blanket spread, ample brownish woolen blanket,
Gray and heavy blanket, folding, covering all.

Curious I halt and silent stand,
Then with light fingers I from the face of the nearest the first
    just lift the blanket;
Who are you elderly man so gaunt and grim, with well-
    gray'd hair, and flesh all sunken about the eyes?
Who are you my dear comrade?

Then to the second I step—and who are you my child and
    darling?
Who are you sweet boy with cheeks yet blooming?

Then to the third—a face nor child nor old, very calm, as of
    beautiful yellow-white ivory;
Young man I think I know you—I think this face is the face of the
    Christ himself,
Dead and divine and brother of all, and here again he lies.

Here is the image of a funeral procession, conceived as a kind of democratic ritual of saying farewell to heroes of the community. If Whitman sometimes uses the expression "en masse," this is perhaps the essence of what he meant by that foreign term.

DIRGE FOR TWO VETERANS

    The last sunbeam
Lightly falls from the finish'd Sabbath,
On the pavement here, and there beyond it is looking,
    Down a new-made double grave.

    Lo, the moon ascending,
Up from the east the silvery round moon,
Beautiful over the house-tops, ghastly, phantom moon,
    Immense and silent moon.

    I see a sad procession,
And I hear the sound of coming full-key'd bugles,
All the channels of the city streets they're flooding,
    As with voices and with tears.

    I hear the great drums pounding,
And the small drums steady whirring,
And every blow of the great convulsive drums,
    Strikes me through and through.

    For the son is brought with the father,
(In the foremost ranks of the fierce assault they fell,
Two veterans son and father dropt together,
    And the double grave awaits them.)

    Now nearer blow the bugles,
And the drums strike more convulsive,
And the daylight o'er the pavement quite has faded,
    And the strong dead-march enwraps me.

In the eastern sky up-buoying,
The sorrowful vast phantom moves illumin'd,
('Tis some mother's large transparent face,
　　In heaven brighter growing.)

　　O strong dead-march you please me!
O moon immense with your silvery face you sooth me!
O my soldiers twain! O my veterans passing to burial!
　　What I have I also give you.

　　The moon gives you light,
And the bugles and the drums give you music,
And my heart, O my soldiers, my veterans,
　　My heart gives you love.

WILLIAM CARLOS WILLIAMS
1883—1963

It is true that William Carlos Williams revolutionized American poetry by intro-
ducing his own form of current speech, based, presumably, on the rhythm of
breathing. However, what is most important is his gift of living among people, the
sympathy and empathy by which he is a sort of successor to Walt Whitman.
Perhaps that is why he chose to be a physician, practicing general medicine in the
town of Rutherford, New Jersey, where he was born. He looked, listened, observed,
and tried to choose the simplest words for his notes on reality.

PROLETARIAN PORTRAIT

A big young bareheaded woman
in an apron

Her hair slicked back standing
on the street

One stockinged foot toeing
the sidewalk

Her shoe in her hand. Looking
intently into it

She pulls out the paper insole
to find the nail

That has been hurting her

TO A POOR OLD WOMAN

munching a plum on
the street a paper bag
of them in her hand

They taste good to her
They taste good
to her. They taste
good to her

You can see it by
the way she gives herself
to the one half
sucked out in her hand

Comforted
a solace of ripe plums
seeming to fill the air
They taste good to her

WANG CHIEN
768—830

If family is a microcosm of society, here we have a glimpse of old Chinese civilization. One can wonder at the stability of such relations as those between the daughter-in-law, the mother-in-law, and the husband's sister. The poem is very vivid and evocative, able to convey a complex relationship in a few lines.

THE NEW WIFE

On the third day she went down to the kitchen,
Washed her hands, prepared the broth.
Still unaware of her new mother's likings,
She asks his sister to taste.

Translated from the Chinese by J. P. Seaton

AL ZOLYNAS
1945—

Al Zolynas, a California poet of Lithuanian origin, teaches in San Diego. This poem is a good example of the bond between teacher and youngsters, though that bond is not always of such intensity.

LOVE IN THE CLASSROOM
—for my students

Afternoon. Across the garden, in Green Hall,
someone begins playing the old piano—
a spontaneous piece, amateurish and alive,
full of a simple, joyful melody.
The music floats among us in the classroom.

I stand in front of my students
telling them about sentence fragments.
I ask them to find the ten fragments
in the twenty-one-sentence paragraph on page forty-five.
They've come from all parts
of the world—Iran, Micronesia, Africa,
Japan, China, even Los Angeles—and they're still
eager to please me. It's less than half
way through the quarter.

They bend over their books and begin.
Hamid's lips move as he follows
the tortuous labyrinth of English syntax.
Yoshie sits erect, perfect in her pale make-up,
legs crossed, quick pulse minutely
jerking her right foot. Tony,
from an island in the South Pacific,
sprawls limp and relaxed in his desk.

The melody floats around and through us
in the room, broken here and there, fragmented,

re-started. It feels mideastern, but
it could be jazz, or the blues—it could be
anything from anywhere.
I sit down on my desk to wait,
and it hits me from nowhere—a sudden
sweet, almost painful love for my students.

"Never mind," I want to cry out.
"It doesn't matter about fragments.
Finding them or not. Everything's
a fragment and everything's not a fragment.
Listen to the music, how fragmented,
how whole, how we can't separate the music
from the sun falling on its knees on all the greenness,
from this movement, how this moment
contains all the fragments of yesterday
and everything we'll ever know of tomorrow!"

Instead, I keep a coward's silence.
the music stops abruptly;
they finish their work,
and we go through the right answers,
which is to say
we separate the fragments from the whole.

RAINER MARIA RILKE
1875—1926

This poem by Rilke narrates the increasing solitude of a person who feels separated from other human beings by her illness. She tries hard not to be left behind, but already her movements show that she is out of step with others. Yet at the same time a transformation is occurring, as if, through her growing blindness, she has moved into another realm.

GOING BLIND

She sat at tea just like the others. First
I merely had a notion that this guest
Held up her cup not quite like all the rest.
And once she gave a smile. It almost hurt.

When they arose at last, with talk and laughter,
And ambled slowly and as chance dictated
Through many rooms, their voices animated,
I saw her seek the noise and follow after,

Held in like one who in a little bit
Would have to sing where many people listened;
Her lighted eyes, which spoke of gladness, glistened
With outward luster, as a pond is lit.

She followed slowly, and it took much trying,
As though some obstacle still barred her stride;
And yet as if she on the farther side
Might not be walking any more, but flying.

Translated from the German by Walter Arndt

LEONARD NATHAN

1924 —

Erotic imagination and disinterested care—how can we separate them? In any case, it is difficult to do so in this poem, the author of which is my colleague and co-translator Leonard Nathan, who lives in Berkeley.

TOAST

There was a woman in Ithaca
who cried softly all night
in the next room and helpless
I fell in love with her under the blanket
of snow that settled on all the roofs
of the town, filling up
every dark depression.

Next morning
in the motel coffee shop
I studied all the made-up faces
of women. Was it the middle-aged blonde
who kidded the waitress
or the young brunette lifting
her cup like a toast?

Love, whoever you are,
your courage was my companion
for many cold towns
after the betrayal of Ithaca,
and when I order coffee
in a strange place, still
I say, lifting, this is for you.

Is it appropriate or inappropriate? Perhaps it's appropriate, since the poet, Leonard Nathan, wrote and published it; and in spite of its joking form, this is a serious poem, sufficiently complex in its thought to discourage us from retelling it in our own words.

BLADDER SONG

On a piece of toilet paper
Afloat in the unflushed piss,
The fully printed lips of a woman.

Nathan, cheer up! The sewer
Sends you a big red kiss.
Ah, nothing's wasted, if it's human.

W. S. MERWIN
1 9 2 7 —

At any moment in our life we are entangled in all the past of humanity, and that
past is primarily language, so we live as if upon a background of incessant chorus,
and of course it is possible to imagine the presence of everything which has ever
been spoken.

UTTERANCE

Sitting over words
very late I have heard a kind of whispered sighing
not far
like a night wind in pines or like the sea in the dark
the echo of everything that has ever
been spoken
still spinning its one syllable
between the earth and silence

STEVE KOWIT

1938—

What does it mean to realize that we are like all our fellow men, that closing ourselves off in our uniqueness, we are wrong, because whatever we feel, others feel too? It means to experience, be it for a moment, but in a truly sharp way, our common fate, the basic and inescapable fact of our mortality. Nothing is more obvious and yet rarely does a poet grasp it as the California poet Steve Kowit has in this joking-serious poem.

NOTICE

This evening, the sturdy Levis
I wore every day for over a year
& which seemed to the end in perfect condition,
suddenly tore.
How or why I don't know,
but there it was—a big rip at the crotch.
A month ago my friend Nick
walked off a racquetball court,
showered,
got into his street clothes,
& halfway home collapsed & died.
Take heed you who read this
& drop to your knees now & again
like the poet Christopher Smart
& kiss the earth & be joyful
& make much of your time
& be kindly to everyone,
even to those who do not deserve it.
For although you may not believe it will happen,
you too will one day be gone.
I, whose Levis ripped at the crotch
for no reason,
assure you that such is the case.
Pass it on.

ANNA SWIR
1909—1984

I have translated a number of poems by Anna Swir (in reality, Anna Swirsz-czynska), because I value her for the intensity and warmth of her poetry, dictated by eros, or by empathy and pity for suffering people. Her poems on war and the Nazi occupation in Poland are among the best in their conciseness. She was also a militant feminist and author of uninhibited love poems.

THE SAME INSIDE

Walking to your place for a love feast
I saw at a street corner
an old beggar woman.

I took her hand,
kissed her delicate cheek,
we talked, she was
the same inside as I am,
from the same kind,
I sensed this instantly
as a dog knows by scent
another dog.

I gave her money,
I could not part from her.
After all, one needs
someone who is close.

And then I no longer knew
why I was walking to your place.

Translated from the Polish by Czeslaw Milosz and Leonard Nathan

PHILIP LARKIN

1922—1985

This is a description of a Dutch painting; it doesn't matter whether as actually seen by the poet, or as a synthetic presentation of those tavern scenes so liked by Dutch painters. Philip Larkin is not a poet especially fond of people. And yet, perhaps, humor gives this poem its grace. It's just humor, not irony or sarcasm, and this is good.

THE CARD-PLAYERS

Jan van Hogspeuw staggers to the door
And pisses at the dark. Outside, the rain
Courses in cart-ruts down the deep mud lane.
Inside, Dirk Dogstoerd pours himself some more,
And holds a cinder to his clay with tongs,
Belching out smoke. Old Prijck snores with the gale,
His skull face firelit; someone behind drinks ale,
And opens mussels, and croaks scraps of songs
Towards the ham-hung rafters about love.
Dirk deals the cards. Wet century-wide trees
Clash in surrounding starlessness above
This lamplit cave, where Jan turns back and farts,
Gobs at the grate, and hits the queen of hearts.

Rain, wind and fire! The secret, bestial peace!

WALT WHITMAN
1819—1892

Some parts of the gigantic oeuvre of Walt Whitman remind me of the huge canvases
of the masters of Renaissance painting. If, looking at those canvases, we direct our
attention to a detail, we discover a multitude of carefully painted small scenes. The
same is true in Whitman: there is something like a mosaic, composed of units that
are autonomous.

FROM "THE SLEEPERS"

Now what my mother told me one day as we sat at dinner
 together,
Of when she was a nearly grown girl living home with her parents
 on the old homestead.

A red squaw came one breakfast-time to the old homestead,
On her back she carried a bundle of rushes for rush-bottoming
 chairs,
Her hair, straight, shiny, coarse, black, profuse, half-envelop'd her
 face,
Her step was free and elastic, and her voice sounded exquisitely as
 she spoke.

My mother look'd in delight and amazement at the stranger,
She look'd at the freshness of her tall-borne face and full and pliant
 limbs,
The more she look'd upon her she loved her,
Never before had she seen such wonderful beauty and purity,
She made her sit on a bench by the jamb of the fireplace, she
 cook'd food for her,
She had no work to give her, but she gave her remembrance and
 fondness.

The red squaw staid all the forenoon, and toward the middle of the
    afternoon she went away,
O my mother was loth to have her go away,
All the week she thought of her, she watch'd for her many a
    month,
She remember'd her many a winter and many a summer,
But the red squaw never came nor was heard of there again.

ANNA SWIR
1909—1984

Anna Swir is the author of a moving cycle of poems about her father and mother, of whom she speaks with attachment and gratitude, which seems to me striking in view of a common tendency, particularly among young poets today, toward just the opposite. It is not without importance to know her biography. She was the only daughter of a painter who was abysmally poor. She grew up in his atelier in Warsaw.

I WASH THE SHIRT

For the last time I wash the shirt
of my father who died.
The shirt smells of sweat. I remember
that sweat from my childhood,
so many years
I washed his shirts and underwear,
I dried them
at an iron stove in the workshop,
he would put them on unironed.

From among all bodies in the world,
animal, human,
only one exuded that sweat.
I breathe it in
for the last time. Washing this shirt
I destroy it
forever.
Now
only paintings survive him
which smell of oils.

Translated from the Polish by Czeslaw Milosz and Leonard Nathan

SHARON OLDS

1943 —

I decided to include this cruel poem for its expressiveness and passion. It appears to deal with a conflict of generations, but in reality it is a dirge for innocence. The daughter knows that her parents are doomed to suffer, but they do not and she looks at them with horror and pity.

I GO BACK TO MAY 1937

I see them standing at the formal gates of their colleges,
I see my father strolling out
under the ochre sandstone arch, the
red tiles glinting like bent
plates of blood behind his head, I
see my mother with a few light books at her hip
standing at the pillar made of tiny bricks with the
wrought-iron gates still open behind her, its
sword-tips black in the May air,
they are about to graduate, they are about to get married,
they are kids, they are dumb, all they know is they are
innocent, they would never hurt anybody.
I want to go up to them and say Stop,
don't do it—she's the wrong woman,
he's the wrong man, you are going to do things
you cannot imagine you would ever do,
you are going to do bad things to children,
you are going to suffer in ways you never heard of,
you are going to want to die. I want to go
up to them there in the late May sunlight and say it,
her hungry pretty blank face turning to me,
her pitiful beautiful untouched body,
his arrogant handsome blind face turning to me
his pitiful beautiful untouched body,
but I don't do it. I want to live. I

take them up like the male and female
paper dolls and bang them together
at the hips like chips of flint as if to
strike sparks from them, I say
Do what you are going to do, and I will tell you about it.

TADEUSZ ROZEWICZ
1921—

A Polish poet, Tadeusz Rozewicz, was marked in his early youth by the cruelties of war, in which he fought against the Nazis as a soldier of a guerilla unit. That experience influenced all his poetry, in which he is a desperate nihilist, but also a compassionate interpreter of the human condition.

A VOICE

They mutilate they torment each other
with silences with words
as if they had another
life to live

they do so
as if they had forgotten
that their bodies
are inclined to death
that the insides of men
easily break down

ruthless with each other
they are weaker
than plants and animals
they can be killed by a word
by a smile by a look

Translated from the Polish by Czeslaw Milosz

Thomas Merton, before he became a monk in a Trappist monastery, Gethsemane,
in Kentucky, had already been a writer, and obviously he respected writers
who shaped the style of his generation. In prose, the srongest influence was
exerted by Ernest Hemingway. When Hemingway killed himself, at the age of
sixty-three, a service for his soul was, for the monk Merton, also a farewell to
his own youth, to his adventurous "I," from which he looked for escape in the
monastery.

AN ELEGY FOR ERNEST HEMINGWAY

Now for the first time on the night of your death
your name is mentioned in convents, *ne cadas in*
obscurum.

Now with a true bell your story becomes final. Now
men in monasteries, men of requiems, familiar with
the dead, include you in their offices.

You stand anonymous among thousands, waiting in
the dark at great stations on the edge of countries
known to prayer alone, where fires are not merciless,
we hope, and not without end.

You pass briefly through our midst. Your books and
writing have not been consulted. Our prayers are
pro defuncto N.

Yet some look up, as though among a crowd of pris-
oners or displaced persons, they recognized a friend
once known in a far country. For these the sun also
rose after a forgotten war upon an idiom you made
great. They have not forgotten you. In their silence
you are still famous, no ritual shade.

How slowly this bell tolls in a monastery tower for a whole age, and for the quick death of an unready dynasty, and for that brave illusion: the adventurous self!

For with one shot the whole hunt is ended!

WALT WHITMAN
1819—1892

I end this chapter with, once again, Whitman. He spins out of himself a thread,
both in his personal life and in his poems, looking for a response, an understanding,
for friends, readers, the perfect opposite of an artist who turns away from people
and the world.

A NOISELESS PATIENT SPIDER

A noiseless patient spider,
I mark'd where on a little promontory it stood isolated,
Mark'd how to explore the vacant vast surrounding,
It launch'd forth filament, filament, filament, out of itself,
Ever reeling them, ever tirelessly speeding them.

And you O my soul where you stand,
Surrounded, detached, in measureless oceans of space,
Ceaselessly musing, venturing, throwing, seeking the spheres
to connect them,
Till the bridge you will need be form'd, till the ductile
anchor hold,
Till the gossamer thread you fling catch somewhere, O my soul.

Woman's Skin

This is a short chapter, perhaps because it should be given to love poetry, and love poetry has always been abundant in any language, so there is no point in adding a few drops to the sea. Besides, it is not poetry written mostly by men that interests me, but something else, woman in her flesh, particularly as described by herself. In some epochs of history women took an active part in literary life and wrote court poetry (in China, in Japan, in France of the sixteenth century). Among them there were great poets, even if they didn't often succeed in breaking with convention and giving voice to their femininity. Today there is a plethora of poems written by women, but I do not find many corresponding to my very specific criteria.

STEVE KOWIT

1938—

Why is the most simple scene of a woman before a mirror a very sensuous poem?
Of course, it's because of a red lip, the tip of the tongue which licks it, and
because of the admiration with which she looks at her eyes.

IN THE MORNING

In the morning,
holding her mirror,
the young woman
touches
her tender
lip with
her finger &
then with
the tip of
her tongue
licks it &
smiles
& admires her
eyes.

        after the Sanskrit

CHU SHU CHEN
c. 1200

*I nearly fell in love with this poet, Chu Shu Chen, about whom not much is known
except that she lived some time around 1200, and one morning suffered because of
her solitude. Reluctantly yet willingly she listened to her servant, who was ready
to enhance her physical charm. The plum flower had a clearly erotic meaning in
that civilization.*

MORNING

I get up. I am sick of
Rouging my cheeks. My face in
The mirror disgusts me. My
Thin shoulders are bowed with
Hopelessness. Tears of loneliness
Well up in my eyes. Wearily
I open my toilet table.
I arch and paint my eyebrows
And steam my heavy braids.
My maid is so stupid that she
Offers me plum blossoms for my hair.

Translated from the Chinese by Kenneth Rexroth

STEVE KOWIT
1938—

The extreme frailty and transience of woman's beauty may give rise to one of those moments when authentic experience overcomes a convention, and this is why poems written about it sound true.

COSMETICS DO NO GOOD

Cosmetics do no good:
no shadow, rouge, mascara, lipstick—
nothing helps.
However artfully I comb my hair,
embellishing my throat & wrists with jewels,
it is no use—there is no
semblance of the beautiful young girl
I was
& long for still.
My loveliness is past.
& no one could be more aware than I am
that coquettishness at this age
only renders me ridiculous.
I know it. Nonetheless,
I primp myself before the glass
like an infatuated schoolgirl
fussing over every detail,
practicing whatever subtlety
may please him.
I cannot help myself.
The God of Passion has his will of me
& I am tossed about
between humiliation & desire,
rectitude & lust,
disintegration & renewal,
ruin & salvation.

after Vidyapati

LI CH'ING-CHAO

1084—1142

Li Ch'ing-chao was once as famous as Li Po and Tu Fu among men. I have read that often in her poems there is a fusion of convention (such as one sees in "the poems of an abandoned concubine") with real experience (the death of her husband).

HOPELESSNESS

When I look in the mirror
My face frightens me.
How horrible I have become!
When Spring comes back
Weakness overcomes me
Like a fatal sickness.
I am too slothful
To smell the new flowers
Or to powder my own face.
Everything exasperates me.
The sadness which tries me today
Adds itself to the accumulated
Sorrows of the days that are gone.
I am frightened by the weird cries
Of the nightjars that I cannot
Shut out from my ears.
I am filled with bitter embarrassment
When I see on the curtains
The shadows of two swallows making love.

Translated from the Chinese by Kenneth Rexroth

ANNA SWIR
1909—1984

Poems about an old woman are rare, as if there were a tendency to relegate her to the realm of half-existence. But Polish poet Anna Swir returns to that subject several times with love and compassion.

THE GREATEST LOVE

She is sixty. She lives
the greatest love of her life.

She walks arm-in-arm with her dear one,
her hair streams in the wind.
Her dear one says:
"You have hair like pearls."

Her children say:
"Old fool."

Translated from the Polish by Czeslaw Milosz and Leonard Nathan

William Blake was inclined to see human sins as phases through which humans pass and not as something substantial. In this poem by Anna Swir there is a similar empathy and forgiveness.

SHE DOES NOT REMEMBER

She was an evil stepmother.
In her old age she is slowly dying
in an empty hovel.

She shudders
like a clutch of burnt paper.
She does not remember that she was evil.
But she knows
that she feels cold.

Translated from the Polish by Czeslaw Milosz and Leonard Nathan

LINDA GREGG
1942—

I consider Linda Gregg one of the best American poets, and I value the neatness
of design in her poems, as well as the energy of each line. Perhaps I am a bit
biased, because Gregg comes from California and used to come to my classes at
the university at Berkeley.

ADULT

I've come back to the country where I was happy
changed. Passion puts no terrible strain on me now.
I wonder what will take the place of desire.
I could be the ghost of my own life returning
to the places I lived best. Walking here and there,
nodding when I see something I cared for deeply.
Now I'm in my house listening to the owls calling
and wondering if slowly I will take on flesh again.

ANNA SWIR
1909—1984

Anna Swir wrote many poems about flesh. I wonder whether she was too brutal for her readers in Poland, or whether her feminism contributed to her being less valued than she should have been. Her love poems are somewhat strange in that they are not confessional.

THANK YOU, MY FATE

Great humility fills me,
great purity fills me,
I make love with my dear
as if I made love dying
as if I made love praying,
tears pour
over my arms and his arms.
I don't know whether this is joy
or sadness, I don't understand
what I feel, I'm crying,
I'm crying, it's humility
as if I were dead,
gratitude, I thank you, my fate,
I'm unworthy, how beautiful
my life.

Translated from the Polish by Czeslaw Milosz and Leonard Nathan

A similar neatness of the calligraphic line depicts lovemaking in the following poem by the same poet. Again, the lovemaking is not that of specific individuals with clearly portrayed faces.

THE SECOND MADRIGAL

A night of love
exquisite as a
concert from old Venice
played on exquisite instruments.
Healthy as a
buttock of a little angel.
Wise as an
anthill.
Garish as air
blown into a trumpet.
Abundant as the reign
of a royal Negro couple
seated on two thrones
cast in gold.

A night of love with you,
a big baroque battle
and two victories.

Translated from the Polish by Czeslaw Milosz and Leonard Nathan

STEVE KOWIT
1938—

In writing about love, there is always the difficulty of crossing a certain line in detailed description. Once, in French love novels, closeness between a man and a woman culminated in "les transports." And that was it, probably more effective than many blatant, detailed descriptions. In this poem, there is something of that discretion.

WHEN HE PRESSED HIS LIPS

When he pressed his lips to my mouth
the knot fell open of itself.
When he pressed them to my throat
the dress slipped to my feet.
So much I know—but
when his lips touched my breast
everything, I swear,
down to his very name,
became so much confused
that I am still,
dear friends,
unable to recount
(as much as I would care to)
what delights
were next bestowed upon me
& by whom.

                after Vikatanitamba

JEAN FOLLAIN
1903—1971

Now, a few poems about women, but not written by women. From time immemorial, femininity was an attribute of nature. The mother earth received the dignity of a goddess in various religions, and was called Gaia by the Greeks; in grammar only the feminine gender fits nature, Ceres, Demeter, Cybele, or Rhea. A woman always was supposed to stand closer to the earth, to maintain permanent union with her, to be her delegate in the world of humans. This poem by a French poet is in that old tradition, which shows, additionally, the ambivalence in men's thinking about women.

A MIRROR

Having gone upstairs
on steps of dark oak
she finds herself before
a mirror with worm-eaten frame
she contemplates in it her virgin torso
all the countryside is ablaze
and gently arrives at her feet
a domestic beast
as if to remind her
of the animal life
which conceals in itself also
the body of a woman.

Translated from the French by Czeslaw Milosz and Robert Hass

EMPEROR CH'IEN-WEN OF LIANG

503—551

There was once an emperor who used to write poems. One day he woke up, opened one eye, and saw that his wife or concubine was getting up and going to make her morning toilet. And he wrote a poem about that, which expresses, let us assume, his wondering about the female species.

GETTING UP IN WINTER

Winter morning.
Pale sunlight strikes the ceiling.
She gets out of bed reluctantly.
Her nightgown has a bamboo sash.
She wipes the dew off her mirror.
At this hour there is no one to see her.
Why is she making up so early?

Translated from the Chinese by Kenneth Rexroth

STEVE KOWIT
1938—

*At least one poem about being charmed by the nakedness of a woman should be
included here.*

WHAT CHORD DID SHE PLUCK

What chord did she pluck in my soul
that girl with the golden necklace
& ivory breasts
whose body ignited the river:
she who rose like the moon
from her bathing &
brushed back the ebony hair
that fell to her waist
& walked off
into the twilight dark—
O my soul,
what chord did she pluck
that I am still trembling.

                    after Chandidas

DENISE LEVERTOV
1923—

Farewells to a body as it once was are like farewells to life. There is a feeling of the abyss of passing time in this poem.

A WOMAN MEETS AN OLD LOVER

'He with whom I ran hand in hand
kicking the leathery leaves down Oak Hill Path
thirty years ago

appeared before me with anxious face, pale,
almost unrecognized, hesitant,
lame.

He whom I cannot remember hearing laugh out loud
but see in mind's eye smiling, self-approving,
wept on my shoulder.

He who seemed always
to take and not give, who took me
so long to forget,

remembered everything I had so long forgotten.'

MAY SWENSON
1919—1989

In this song directed to her body, May Swenson writes about a peculiar relationship
to it. She is not identical with it but is the owner of it. The body is her house,
her horse, her hound, and death is like exposure and poverty.

QUESTION

Body my house
my horse my hound
what will I do
when you are fallen

Where will I sleep
How will I ride
What will I hunt

Where can I go
without my mount
all eager and quick
How will I know
in thicket ahead
is danger or treasure
when Body my good
bright dog is dead

How will it be
to lie in the sky
without roof or door
and wind for an eye
With cloud for shift
how will I hide?

ROBINSON JEFFERS
1887—1962

In this poem, a woman speaks, but what she says is related by a man. This is one of Robinson Jeffers' late poems, and even a cursory knowledge of his biography suffices to recognize the voice of Una Custer, Jeffers' wife, with whom he'd lived in Carmel since his youth.

CREMATION

It nearly cancels my fear of death, my dearest said,
When I think of cremation. To rot in the earth
Is a loathsome end, but to roar up in flame—besides, I
        am used to it,
I have flamed with love or fury so often in my life,
No wonder my body is tired, no wonder it is dying.
We had great joy of my body. Scatter the ashes.

TADEUSZ ROZEWICZ
1921—

This poem by Tadeusz Rozewicz is about absence, but just as in Samuel Beckett, absence expresses something that is not attainable, yet nevertheless exists. And so love, here, is defined only negatively.

A SKETCH FOR A MODERN LOVE POEM

And yet whiteness
can be best described by greyness
a bird by a stone
sunflowers
in december

love poems of old
used to be descriptions of flesh
they described this and that
for instance eyelashes

and yet redness
should be described
by greyness the sun by rain
the poppies in november
the lips at night

the most palpable
description of bread
is that of hunger
there is in it
a humid porous core
a warm inside
sunflowers at night
the breasts the belly the thighs of Cybele

a transparent
source-like description
of water is that of thirst

of ash
of desert
it provokes a mirage
clouds and trees enter
a mirror of water
lack hunger
absence
of flesh
is a description of love
in a modern love poem

Translated from the Polish by Czeslaw Milosz

ANNA SWIR
1909—1984

A few centuries ago European poetry counted a number of poems on the dialogue between the soul and the body. This genre still exists, and here, in "I Talk to My Body" by Anna Swir, it is modified into the tender-humorous conversation of a woman with her cherished possession.

I TALK TO MY BODY

My body, you are an animal
whose appropriate behavior
is concentration and discipline.
An effort
of an athlete, of a saint and of a yogi.

Well trained
you may become for me
a gate
through which I will leave myself
and a gate
through which I will enter myself.
A plumb line to the center of the earth
and a cosmic ship to Jupiter.

My body, you are an animal
for whom ambition
is right.
Splendid possibilities
are open to us.

Translated from the Polish by Czeslaw Milosz and Leonard Nathan

TROUBLES WITH THE SOUL
AT MORNING CALISTHENICS

Lying down I lift my legs,
my soul by mistake jumps into my legs.
This is not convenient for her,
besides, she must branch,
for the legs are two.

When I stand on my head
my soul sinks down to my head.
She is then in her place.

But how long can you stand on your head,
especially if you do not know
how to stand on your head.

Translated from the Polish by Czeslaw Milosz and Leonard Nathan

And yet, a humorous poem written by a man addressing his belly couldn't have been written. A woman's belly is something very different emotionally. In any case, it is a proper partner for conversation.

I STARVE MY BELLY FOR A SUBLIME PURPOSE

Three days
I starve my belly
so that it learns
to eat the sun.

I say to it: Belly,
I am ashamed of you. You must
spiritualize yourself. You must
eat the sun.

The belly keeps silent
for three days. It's not easy
to waken in it higher aspirations.

Yet I hope for the best.
This morning, tanning myself on the beach,
I noticed that, little by little,
it begins to shine.

Translated from the Polish by Czeslaw Milosz and Leonard Nathan

Situations

The diversity and multicolored richness of life come to a large extent from the innumerable situations in which we participate, being born at a given time, in a given country, into such and not other traditions and mores. And, above all, from our memory, and not only our own memory, for we are like a thread in a huge fabric of generations. That fabric today extends more and more, for knowledge of history and of the literature and art of other civilizations increases, and roads are open for travelling through centuries and millennia. In this chapter I place just some samples, though imagination suggests a multitude of "situational" poems.

TU FU

713—770

*Divertissements from over a thousand years ago—so similar to ours that they provoke
a feeling of solidarity, because they are, like ours, dependent on good weather, and
we take pity on those girls whose makeup has been ruined.*

DEJEUNER SUR L'HERBE

I
It's pleasant to board the ferry in the sunscape
As the late light slants into afternoon;
The faint wind ruffles the river, rimmed with foam.
We move through the aisles of bamboo
Towards the cool water-lilies.

The young dandies drop ice into the drinks,
While the girls slice the succulent lotus root.
Above us, a patch of cloud spreads, darkening
Like a water-stain on silk.

Write this down quickly, before the rain!

Don't sit there! The cushions were soaked by the shower.
Already the girls have drenched their crimson skirts.
Beauties, their powder streaked with mascara,
    lament their ruined faces.

The wind batters our boat, the mooring-line
Has rubbed a wound in the willow bark.
The edges of the curtains are embroidered by the river foam.
Like a knife in a melon, Autumn slices Summer.

It will be cold, going back.

Translated from the Chinese by Carolyn Kizer

JOANNE KYGER
1934—

I think that poems about situations could be drawn from a hat, relying upon chance,
which would correspond to their nature, as they are somehow related to chance.
Here we have Bolinas, a small town on the Pacific shore north of San Francisco,
very quiet and once willingly chosen by hippies. Joanne Kyger, who lives there,
practicing meditation, we learn, touches upon quite a problem. "Cessation of per-
sonality" is desirable but also dangerous.

AND WITH MARCH A DECADE IN BOLINAS

Just sitting around smoking, drinking and telling stories,
the news, making plans, analyzing, approaching the cessation
of personality, the single personality understands its demise.
Experience of the simultaneity of all human beings on this planet,
alive when you are alive. This seemingly inexhaustible
sophistication of awareness becomes relentless and horrible,
trapped. How am I ever going to learn enough to get out.

The beautiful soft and lingering props of the Pacific here.

          The back door bangs
      So we've made a place to live
  here in the greened out 70's
            Trying to talk in the Tremulous
        morality of the present
    Great Breath, I give you, Great Breath!

ALEKSANDER WAT
1900—1967

Hamlet exists in the consciousness of poets, otherwise such a poem as this one couldn't have been written. It is a text embroidering upon a text, upon the story of Hamlet, his mother, and Ophelia. Not by accident, this poem is dedicated to E. G. Craig, a great reformer of the theater in England. Craig had a long life. Wat met him in the south of France.

A JOKE
To Gordon Craig

Bunches of carnations in a tin pitcher.
Beyond the window, is that a faun playing a flute?
In a fusty room the semi-darkness of dawn.
The lovers sleep. On the sill

the cat purrs. In its dream a rabble of birds.
She wakens like a bird and, trembling,
opens her eye on the alabaster
shaded mournfully by her streaming hair.

She found in it her wreath fished up from a river
and searches for his hand, looking for protection.
Then plunges into sleep again—into a flow, a flow . . .

Suddenly the door creaked softly. Somebody enters. Surprised
Looks, hardly believes: My son—with a woman!
and retreats on tiptoe: O Hamlet! Hamlet!

VENCE, SEPTEMBER 1956

Translated from the Polish by Czeslaw Milosz and Leonard Nathan

PO CHÜ-I
772—846

Po Chü-I read and respected philosophers. Some people called him a Taoist. Never-
theless, he allowed himself malice in addressing a legendary sage, the creator of
Taoism. Let us concede that it's a difficult problem, discovered by similar poets who
announce the end of poetry, and yet continue writing.

THE PHILOSOPHERS:
LAO-TZU

"Those who speak know nothing:
Those who know are silent."
Those words, I am told,
Were spoken by Lao-tzu,
If we are to believe that Lao-tzu,
    Was himself one who knew,
How comes it that he wrote a book
    Of five thousand words?

Translated from the Chinese by Arthur Waley

This is Po Chü-I's poem about one of his troubles. Perhaps it doesn't concern us much, but let us only imagine: we make preparations for departure from the city, retiring to the house we had built in the mountains, and suddenly all this comes to nothing.

GOLDEN BELLS

    When I was almost forty
I had a daughter whose name was Golden Bells.
Now it is just a year since she was born;
She is learning to sit and cannot yet talk.
Ashamed—to find that I have not a sage's heart;
I cannot resist vulgar thoughts and feelings.
Henceforward I am tied to things outside myself;
My only reward—the pleasure I am getting now.
If I am spared the grief of her dying young,
Then I shall have the trouble of getting her married.
My plan for retiring and going back to the hills
Must now be postponed for fifteen years!

Translated from the Chinese by Arthur Waley

A considerable number of Chinese poems in my collection can be explained as my attempt to jump over the barrier built by time between them and us. In this I behave like many of my contemporaries who discover that what had been, until recently, the trappings of exoticism has masked the eternal man.

AFTER GETTING DRUNK, BECOMING SOBER IN THE NIGHT

Our party scattered at yellow dusk and I came home to bed;
I woke at midnight and went for a walk, leaning heavily on a
 friend.
As I lay on my pillow my vinous complexion, soothed by sleep,
 grew sober:
In front of the tower the ocean moon, accompanying the tide, had
 risen.
The swallows, about to return to the beams, went back to roost
 again;
The candle at my window, just going out, suddenly revived its
 light.
All the time till dawn came, still my thoughts were muddled;
And in my ears something sounded like the music of flutes and
 strings.

Translated from the Chinese by Arthur Waley

WAYNE DODD
1930—

Rural America persists in the consciousness of city inhabitants, for after all many of them have come from families with a rural background. Here, the news of a farmer's death brings members of the family from a distant city.

OF HIS LIFE

Beside the gravel pile, the lizard
warms himself in the dazzling greenness
of his life, watching us casually
through half-lidded eyes.
It is May.
Next week he would have been 57.
My daughter holds my hand, 3 years old
and ignorant, the airsickness forgotten,
and the hurried trip
and interrupted sleep.
Below the road
the whiteface cattle graze
in the morning peace.
The house is quiet.
Inside, his daughters stare unbelieving
into coffee cups, unable to imagine
the future.
My child throws some gravel
and the lizard fixes us
with both eyes, but does not
run, unwilling to leave
the warmth of the sun.
I can hear everything so clearly.
Years later she will ask
what he was like, her grandfather.
And I will try to remember
the greenness of this lizard,
he loved the sun so.

RAYMOND CARVER
1938—1988

Raymond Carver was one of the best-known American short-story writers, but also an excellent poet. Death from cancer interrupted his work at a moment of full development, after he had overcome his alcoholism. I couldn't read this poem on Alexander the Great without thinking of his biography, to which, besides, he refers.

WINE

Reading a life of Alexander the Great, Alexander
whose rough father, Philip, hired Aristotle to tutor
the young scion and warrior, to put some polish
on his smooth shoulders. Alexander who, later
on the campaign trail into Persia, carried a copy of
The Iliad in a velvet-lined box, he loved that book so
much. He loved to fight and drink, too.
I came to that place in the life where Alexander, after
a long night of carousing, a wine-drunk (the worst kind of drunk—
hangovers you don't forget), threw the first brand
to start a fire that burned Persepolis, capital of the Persian Empire
(ancient even in Alexander's day).
Razed it right to the ground. Later, of course,
next morning—maybe even while the fire roared—he was
remorseful. But nothing like the remorse felt
the next evening when, during a disagreement that turned ugly
and, on Alexnder's part, overbearing, his face flushed
from too many bowls of uncut wine, Alexander rose drunkenly to
    his feet,
grabbed a spear and drove it through the breast
of his friend, Cletus, who'd saved his life at Granicus.
For three days Alexander mourned. Wept. Refused food. "Refused
to see to his bodily needs." He even promised
to give up wine forever.
(I've heard such promises and the lamentations that go with them.)
Needless to say, life for the army came to a full stop

as Alexander gave himself over to his grief.
But at the end of those three days, the fearsome heat
beginning to take its toll on the body of his dead friend,
Alexander was persuaded to take action. Pulling himself together
and leaving his tent, he took out his copy of Homer, untied it,
began to turn the pages. Finally he gave orders that the funeral
rites described for Patroklos be followed to the letter:
he wanted Cletus to have the biggest possible send-off.
And when the pyre was burning and the bowls of wine were
passed his way during the ceremony? Of course, what do you
think? Alexander drank his fill and passed
out. He had to be carried to his tent. He had to be lifted, to be put
into his bed.

FRANZ WRIGHT
1953—

This is a situation about which we read, and which presumably had been fixed in a painting by Picasso as well.

DEPICTION OF CHILDHOOD
After Picasso

It is the little girl
guiding the minotaur
with her free hand—
that devourer

and all the terror he's accustomed to
effortlessly emanating,
his ability to paralyze
merely by becoming present,

entranced somehow, and transformed
into a bewildered
and who knows, grateful
gentleness . . .

and with the other hand
lifting her lamp.

JAMES TATE
1943—

James Tate's poem is, to some extent, a satire on the profession of writing, and a connection between self-love and the urge to create.

TEACHING THE APE TO WRITE

They didn't have much trouble
teaching the ape to write poems:
first they strapped him into the chair
then tied his pencil around his hand
(the paper had already been nailed down).
Then Dr. Bluespire leaned over his shoulder
and whispered into his ear:
"You look like a god sitting there.
Why don't you try writing something?"

WISLAWA SZYMBORSKA
1923—

Writing is a vocation but many writers experience it also as a curse and a burden.
In a way, they feel as if they are serving as instruments to a force alien to them.
But writing, be it a blessing or a curse, may also be treated humorously by its
practitioners, and in this amusing verse the word "poems" at the end of the lines
serves to enhance the weirdness of that occupation.

IN PRAISE OF MY SISTER

My sister does not write poems
and it's unlikely she'll suddenly start writing poems.
She takes after her mother, who did not write poems,
and after her father, who also did not write poems.
Under my sister's roof I feel safe:
nothing would move my sister's husband to write poems.
And though it sounds like a poem by Adam Macedoński,
none of my relatives is engaged in the writing of poems.

In my sister's desk there are no old poems
nor any new ones in her handbag.
And when my sister invites me to dinner,
I know she has no intention of reading me poems.
She makes superb soups without half trying,
and her coffee does not spill on manuscripts.

In many families no one writes poems,
but when they do, it's seldom just one person.
Sometimes poetry flows in cascades of generations,
which sets up fearsome eddies in family relations.

My sister cultivates a decent spoken prose,
her entire literary output is on vacation postcards
that promise the same thing every year:
that when she returns,
she'll tell us, everything,
everything,
everything.

Translated from the Polish by Magnus J. Krynski and Robert A. Maguire

LAWRENCE RAAB
1946—

The frailty of so-called civilized life, our awareness that it lasts merely by a miracle, because at any moment it could disintegrate and reveal unmitigated horror, as has happened more than once in our century—all this could contribute to the writing of this poem. Its author lives in an idyllic New England, and has a window with a view of an orchard.

SUDDEN APPEARANCE OF A MONSTER AT A WINDOW

Yes, his face really is so terrible
you cannot turn away. And only
that thin sheet of glass between you,
clouding with his breath.
Behind him: the dark scribbles of trees
in the orchard, where you walked alone
just an hour ago, after the storm had passed,
watching water drip from the gnarled branches,
stepping carefully over the sodden fruit.
At any moment he could put his fist
right through that window. And on your side:
you could grab hold of this
letter opener, or even now try
very slowly to slide the revolver
out of the drawer of the desk in front of you.
But none of this will happen. And not because
you feel sorry for him, or detect
in his scarred face some helplessness
that shows in your own as compassion.
You will never know what he wanted,
what he might have done, since
this thing, of its own accord, turns away.
And because yours is a life in which

such a monster cannot figure for long,
you compose yourself, and return
to your letter about the storm, how it bent
the apple trees so low they dragged
on the ground, ruining the harvest.

TU FU
713—770

I have yet two Chinese poems, one of which is about meeting a monster, though not that dangerous, because it's only a tiger. It seems that in old China, at least in some provinces, such a meeting was not a rarity.

COMING HOME LATE AT NIGHT

At midnight, coming home, I passed a tiger.
The mountain's black, inside they're all asleep.
Far off the Dipper lowers toward the River.
Above, Bright Star grows great upon the sky.
With candle in the court I glower at two flames.
The apes are restive in the gorge, I hear one cry.
White head, old no more, I dance and sing.
Lean on my cane, unsleeping. And what else!

Translated from the Chinese by J. P. Seaton

*The situation of amassed adversity—winter, evening, solitude, old age—can some-
times so depress that even a poet sure of himself feels the uselessness of writing.
Those of us who have experienced such evenings will recognize ourselves in that
voice.*

SNOW STORM

Tumult, weeping, many new ghosts.
Heartbroken, aging, alone, I sing
To myself. Ragged mist settles
In the spreading dusk. Snow scurries
In the coiling wind. The wineglass
Is spilled. The bottle is empty.
The fire has gone out in the stove.
Everywhere men speak in whispers.
I brood on the uselessness of letters.

Translated from the Chinese by Kenneth Rexroth

BRONISLAW MAJ
1953 —

An unrepeatable situation. Only this, and not another man, so this and not another
leaf. Which means that one can practice a philosophical poetry not using the dry
terms of philosophy.

A LEAF

A leaf, one of the last, parts from a maple branch:
it is spinning in the transparent air of October, falls
on a heap of others, stops, fades. No one
admired its entrancing struggle with the wind,
followed its flight, no one will distinguish it now
as it lies among other leaves, no one saw
what I did. I am
the only one.

Translated from the Polish by Czeslaw Milosz and Robert Hass

ANNA SWIR
1909—1984

Poetry readings are not common in some countries. In others, among them Poland,
they draw an audience that doesn't treat poetry as an aesthetic experience only.
Rather, in one way or another, such audiences bring to the event their multiple
questions about life and death. This poem captures well the ignorance and help-
lessness of both the poet and her listeners.

POETRY READING

I'm curled into a ball
like a dog
that is cold.

Who will tell me
why I was born,
why this monstrosity
called life.

The telephone rings. I have to give
a poetry reading.

I enter.
A hundred people, a hundred pairs of eyes.
They look, they wait.
I know for what.

I am supposed to tell them
why they were born,
why there is
this monstrosity called life.

Translated from the Polish by Czeslaw Milosz and Leonard Nathan

Nonattachment

The futility of human endeavors, the fleetingness of human life, limited to a brief span of time, is a perennial subject of meditation in Babylonian poetry, in the Bible, in Greek tragedy, in Latin poets. The "vanity of vanities" of Ecclesiastes sets the tone for writings in Judeo-Christian civilization, otherwise so aggressive and grabbing. Nonattachment to the turmoil of daily strivings is advocated by prophets and saints. In the twentieth century, the meeting of civilizations, East and West, brings together biblical wisdom, Taoism, Buddhism, and Sufism in common praise of a detached attitude as a prerequisite for enlightenment.

Vita activa, an active life, or *vita contemplativa,* the contemplative life? Which to choose? That dilemma, formulated in medieval Europe and reflecting the polarity of the knight's and the monk's ways of life, is also present in old Chinese poetry. Poets were usually officials on various levels of the state bureaucracy, but they were perfectly aware of the merely relative value of riches and dignities. In many poems they hesitate between their desire to pursue a career and to retire to the country, far from the court and the market. Poetry was written by emperors as well. They had limited possibility of choice, except to peserve their nonattachment while occupying the throne.

This perennial theme is so essential for poetry that it has been molded into newer and newer forms.

RAYMOND CARVER
1938—1988

The most classical poem of nonattachment is that of a sudden realization, in a flash, of the shortness of the time one has left to live.

THE COBWEB

A few minutes ago, I stepped onto the deck
of the house. From there I could see and hear the water,
and everything that's happened to me all these years.
It was hot and still. The tide was out.
No birds sang. As I leaned against the railing
a cobweb touched my forehead.
It caught in my hair. No one can blame me that I turned
and went inside. There was no wind. The sea was
dead calm. I hung the cobweb from the lampshade.
Where I watch it shudder now and then when my breath
touches it. A fine thread. Intricate.
Before long, before anyone realizes,
I'll be gone from here.

DENISE LEVERTOV
1923—

A slow maturing, long awaited, probably identical with prayer, sometimes called by the mystics "the night of the soul" can, in modern poetry, take the lay form of a black eye mask.

EYE MASK

In this dark I rest,
unready for the light which dawns
day after day,
eager to be shared.
Black silk, shelter me.
I need
more of the night before I open
eyes and heart
to illumination. I must still
grow in the dark like a root
not ready, not ready at all.

PO CHÜ-I
771–846

One moment of nonattachment, of meditation, and, immediately following, the return
of a high official, as we guess, to court intrigue and commercial transaction.

CLIMBING THE LING-YING TERRACE
AND LOOKING NORTH

Mounting on high I begin to realize the smallness of Man's
    Domain;
Gazing into the distance I begin to know the vanity of the Carnal
    World.
I turn my head and hurry home——back to the Court and Market,
A single grain of rice falling——in the Great Barn.

Translated from the Chinese by Arthur Waley

ESKIMO (ANONYMOUS)

An Eskimo poet, who will forever remain anonymous, composed a song based on a legend of origins from the oral tradition.

MAGIC WORDS

In the very earliest time,
when both people and animals lived on earth,
a person could become an animal if he wanted to
and an animal could become a human being.
Sometimes they were people
and sometimes animals
and there was no difference.
All spoke the same language.
That was the time when words were like magic.
The human mind had mysterious powers.
A word spoken by chance
might have strange consequences.
It would suddenly come alive
and what people wanted to happen could
         happen—
all you had to do was say it.
Nobody could explain this:
That's the way it was.

Translated from the Inuit by Edward Field

NACHMAN OF BRATZLAV
1771—1810

And why after all does the world exist? That was the subject of a Hasid, Nachman of Bratzlav. And he tried, as did his predecessor of the sixteenth century, the master of the Kabbalah, Isaac Luria, to answer the question: How is it possible that the Highest, who fills everything that exists with Himself, could create the universe, which is not He?

FROM "THE TORAH OF THE VOID"

God,
for Mercy's sake,
created the world
to reveal Mercy.
If there were no world
on whom would Mercy take pity?

So—to show His Mercy
He created the worlds
from *Aziluth*'s peak
to this Earth's center.

But as He wished to create
there was not a *where*?
All was Infinitely He,
Be He Blessed!

The light He condensed
sideways
thus was *space* made
an empty void.

In *space* days and measures
came into being.
So the world was created.

This void was needed
for the world's sake,
so that it may be
put into place.

Don't strain to understand
this void!
It is a mystery—not to be realized
until the future
is the *now*.

       ★

Once there was *light*,
much and powerful,
holy *light*,
and it was in vessels
—too much *light*,
too much power—
and the *vessels* burst!

When the *vessels* burst
the fragments
of Holiness
took form
becoming the *outered* sciences.

So, even of Holiness
there is offal:
Just as there is sweat
and hair and excrement,
so Holiness too
has its offal.

Translated from the Hebrew by Zalman Schachter

JELALUDDIN RUMI
1207—1273

We know as much about the beginning and the end, about the infinite complexity
of the world, as does an embryo locked in its mother's womb. This parable by a
Persian poet-mystic, making use of that metaphor, calls for our opening up to that
whole dimension of existence which escapes our words.

Little by little, wean yourself.

This is the gist of what I have to say.

From an embryo, whose nourishment comes in the blood,
move to an infant drinking milk,
to a child on solid food,
to a searcher after wisdom,
to a hunter of more invisible game.

Think how it is to have a conversation with an embryo.
You might say, "The world outside is vast and intricate.
There are wheatfields and mountain passes, and orchards in bloom.

At night there are millions of galaxies, and in sunlight
the beauty of friends dancing at a wedding."

You ask the embryo why he, or she, stays cooped up
in the dark with eyes closed.

Listen to the answer.

There is no "other world."
I only know what I've experienced.
You must be hallucinating.

Mathnawi, III, 49—6

Translated from the Persian by Coleman Barks

W. S. MERWIN
1927 —

*The following poem inspires us to reflect on what seldom crosses our minds. After
all (literally after all), such an anniversary awaits every one of us.*

FOR THE ANNIVERSARY OF MY DEATH

Every year without knowing it I have passed the day
When the last fires will wave to me
And the silence will set out
Tireless traveler
Like the beam of a lightless star

Then I will no longer
Find myself in life as in a strange garment
Surprised at the earth
And the love of one woman
And the shamelessness of men
As today writing after three days of rain
Hearing the wren sing and the falling cease
And bowing not knowing to what

YORUBA TRIBE

In African folklore, I have found a strange image of the Creator as a swarm of bees.

INVOCATION OF THE CREATOR

He is patient, he is not angry.
He sits in silence to pass judgment.
He sees you even when he is not looking.
He stays in a far place—but his eyes are on the town.

He stands by his children and lets them succeed.
He causes them to laugh—and they laugh.
Ohoho—the father of laughter.
His eye is full of joy.
He rests in the sky like a swarm of bees.

Obatala—who turns blood into children.

Translated by Ulli Beier

CHUANG TZU
3rd—4th century B.C.

Masters of nonattachment, the Chinese Taoists would give first of all practical advice—advice of the Way, for such is the literal meaning of the word Tao, though it means much more and that is why it is untranslatable.

MAN IS BORN IN TAO

Fishes are born in water
Man is born in Tao.
If fishes, born in water,
Seek the deep shadow
Of pond and pool,
All their needs
Are satisfied.
If man, born in Tao,
Sinks into the deep shadow
Of non-action
To forget aggression and concern,
He lacks nothing
His life is secure.

Moral: "All the fish needs
Is to get lost in water.
All man needs is to get lost
In Tao."

Translated from the Chinese by Thomas Merton

Nonacting is not the same as passivity. But energy alone is not everything, and sometimes, when we strive incessantly, we achieve an outcome just opposite to what was intended—we learn from the same Chuang Tzu.

THE NEED TO WIN

When an archer is shooting for nothing
He has all his skill.
If he shoots for a brass buckle
He is already nervous.
If he shoots for a prize of gold
He goes blind
Or sees two targets—
He is out of his mind!

His skill has not changed. But the prize
Divides him. He cares.
He thinks more of winning
Than of shooting—
And the need to win
Drains him of power.

Translated from the Chinese by Thomas Merton

JELALUDDIN RUMI
1207—1273

*Because the question of good and evil has been tormenting us since the moment we
plucked a fruit from the tree of knowledge, perhaps it's worthwhile to remind
ourselves that there have been people who didn't take to heart that pair of opposite
notions. For them, as for Jelaluddin Rumi, nonattachment meant simply that you
could lie down in a meadow.*

Out beyond ideas of wrongdoing and rightdoing,
there is a field. I'll meet you there.

When the soul lies down in that grass,
the world is too full to talk about.
Ideas, language, even the phrase *each other*
doesn't make any sense.

Translated by Coleman Barks and John Moyne

LI PO
701—762

Perhaps in this Chinese poem there is something similar to the poem by Rumi.
Motionless sitting and meditating on a landscape leads to the disappearance of our
separate existence, so we become the mountain we contemplate.

THE BIRDS HAVE VANISHED

The birds have vanished into the sky,
and now the last cloud drains away.

We sit together, the mountain and me,
until only the mountain remains.

Translated from the Chinese by Sam Hamill

DENISE LEVERTOV
1923—

Original sin doesn't leave us in peace, for it is enigmatic, if only because the distinction between good and evil is connected with the faculty of reason and with Satan's promise that "you will be like gods." Denise Levertov writes a poem of our repentance.

CONTRABAND

The tree of knowledge was the tree of reason.
That's why the taste of it
drove us from Eden. That fruit
was meant to be dried and milled to a fine powder
for use a pinch at a time, a condiment.
God had probably planned to tell us later
about this new pleasure.
                    We stuffed our mouths full of it,
gorged on *but* and *if* and *how* and again
but, knowing no better.
It's toxic in large quantities; fumes
swirled in our heads and around us
to form a dense cloud that hardened to steel,
a wall between us and God, Who was Paradise.
Not that God is unreasonable—but reason
in such excess was tyranny
and locked us into its own limits, a polished cell
reflecting our own faces. God lives
on the other side of that mirror,
but through the slit where the barrier doesn't
quite touch ground, manages still
to squeeze in—as filtered light,
splinters of fire, a strain of music heard
then lost, then heard again.

CH'ANG YU
c. 810

In poets of Asia, we often find the theme of liberation from "earthly ties," conceived as our participation in human society. Even emperors are not free from that strife.

A RINGING BELL

I lie in my bed,
Listening to the monastery bell.
In the still night
The sound re-echoes amongst the hills.
Frost gathers under the cold moon.
Under the overcast sky,
In the depths of the night,
The first tones are still reverberating
While the last tones are ringing clear and sharp.
I listen and I can still hear them both,
But I cannot tell when they fade away.
I know the bondage and vanity of the world.
But who can tell when we escape
From life and death?

Translated from the Chinese by Kenneth Rexroth

WANG WEI

701—761

*Wang Wei was a poet and a painter but also an official, and many of his poems
juxtapose contemplative life in the spirit of Taoism and Buddhism with active life
and career from which it's not easy to be liberated. But in his old age he achieved
a peculiar kind of nonattachment, when even poetry and painting seemed to him too
close to earthly delusions.*

LAZY ABOUT WRITING POEMS

With time I become lazy about writing poems.
Now my only company is old age.
In an earlier life I was a poet, a mistake,
and my former body belonged to a painter.
I can't abandon habits of that life
and sometimes am recognized by people of this world.
My name and pen name speak my former being
but about all this my heart is ignorant.

Translated from the Chinese by Tony and Willis Barnstone and Xu Haixin

If one lost the game, if one's political foes were effectively undermining one and at last triumphed, it was necessary to withdraw somewhere, to a house in the mountains, at least temporarily. Unfortunately, such a thing could hardly be done temporarily, and one had to accept that it would be forever. White clouds have the symbolic meaning of a world beyond and of the contemplation of things eternal.

A FAREWELL

I dismount from my horse and drink your wine.
I ask where you're going
You say you are a failure
and want to hibernate at the foot of Deep South Mountain.
Once you're gone no one will ask about you.
There are endless white clouds on the mountain.

Translated from the Chinese by Tony and Willis Barnstone and Xu Haixin

To be free, at least for a short time, to forget about the court and the market, as here, in a boat on the lake.

DRIFTING ON THE LAKE

Autumn is crisp and the firmament far,
especially far from where people live.
I look at cranes on the sand
and am immersed in joy when I see mountains beyond
      the clouds.
Dusk inks the crystal ripples.
Leisurely the white moon comes out.
Tonight I am with my oar, alone, and can do
      everything,
yet waver, not willing to return.

Translated from the Chinese by Tony and Willis Barnstone and Xu Haixin

TU FU

713—770

The bucolic theme seems to be present in practically all Chinese poets, and of course in the most famous, Tu Fu.

VISITORS

I have had asthma for a
Long time. It seems to improve
Here in this house by the river.
It is quiet too. No crowds
Bother me. I am brighter
And more rested. I am happy here.
When someone calls at my thatched hut
My son brings me my straw hat
And I go out and gather
A handful of fresh vegetables.
It isn't much to offer.
But it is given in friendship.

Translated from the Chinese by Kenneth Rexroth

PO CHÜ-I
772—846

*Let us say, though, that there is a backstage to that praise of the healthy peasant
life. Poets belonged to the caste of the educated, and could sometimes idealize the
country and yokels who worked the soil, but it was not their milieu. Whether they
were building their villas among the vineyards, like Roman poets, houses in the
mountains, like the Chinese, or dachas, like the Russians, they were always aware
of a distance. And especially in China, where the literate had to pass numerous
and difficult state examinations.*

LODGING WITH THE OLD MAN OF THE STREAM

Men's hearts love gold and jade;
Men's mouths covet wine and flesh.
Not so the old man of the stream;
He drinks from his gourd and asks nothing more.
South of the stream he cuts firewood and grass;
North of the stream he has built wall and roof.
Yearly he sows a single acre of land;
In spring he drives two yellow calves.
In these things he finds great repose;
Beyond these he has no wish or care.
By chance I met him walking by the water-side;
He took me home and lodged me in his thatched hut.
When I parted from him, to seek Market and Court,
This old man asked my rank and pay.
Doubting my tale, he laughed loud and long:
"Privy Counsellors do not sleep in barns."

Translated from the Chinese by Arthur Waley

MIRON BIALOSZEWSKI
1922—1983

Miron Bialoszewski was a poet of Warsaw, rooted in the city's folklore and ex-
perimenting with street slang. He survived the complete ruin of his city, first in
the German action against the Jewish ghetto, then in the uprising of 1944. Not
similar in his writings to any of his contemporaries, he could have been the epitome
of the nonattachment achieved by some Taoists, although in him, it was spontaneous,
not programmatic. And he was a humorous poet, describing the most ordinary human
actions with an attention deserved by much greater events.

A BALLAD OF GOING DOWN TO THE STORE

First I went down to the street
by means of the stairs,
just imagine it,
by means of the stairs.

Then people known to people unknown
passed me by and I passed them by.
Regret
that you did not see
how people walk,
regret!

I entered a complete store:
lamps of glass were glowing.
I saw somebody—he sat down—
and what did I hear? what did I hear?
rustling of bags and human talk.

And indeed,
indeed,
I returned.

Translated from the Polish by Czeslaw Milosz

MUSO SOSEKI
1275—1351

Nonattachment and liberation are, in poetry, often associated with old age because the years bring—in any case, they should bring—some wisdom, as in this poem by a Japanese poet.

OLD MAN AT LEISURE

Sacred or secular
    manners and conventions
        make no difference to him
Completely free
    leaving it all to heaven
        he seems a simpleton
No one catches
    a glimpse inside
        his mind
this old man
    all by himself
        between heaven and earth

Translated from the Japanese by W. S. Merwin

KENNETH REXROTH
1905—1982

Kenneth Rexroth, who used to live in Japan, wrote toward the end of his life a
parable on Buddha, a poem of far-reaching nonattachment.

FROM "THE CITY OF THE MOON"

Buddha took some Autumn leaves
In his hand and asked
Ananda if these were all
The red leaves there were.
Ananda answered that it
Was Autumn and leaves
Were falling all about them,
More than could ever
Be numbered. So Buddha said,
"I have given you
A handful of truths. Besides
These there are many
Thousands of other truths, more
Than can ever be numbered."

This poem may be considered as a last testament of Rexroth's.

A LONG LIFETIME

A long lifetime
Peoples and places
And the crisis of mankind—
What survives is the crystal—
Infinitely small—
Infinitely large—

SOUTHERN BUSHMEN

In this Bushmen's song, there is a note of concern and lament, but probably it's more expressive of a serene acceptance of the immutable order of the world.

THE DAY WE DIE

The day we die
the wind comes down
to take away
our footprints.

The wind makes dust
to cover up
the marks we left
while walking.

For otherwise
the thing would seem
as if we were
still living.

Therefore the wind
is he who comes
to blow away
our footprints.

ANNA KAMIEŃSKA
[dates unknown]

Anna Kamieńska was a Christian deeply living both the Old Testament and the New Testament. In her old age she achieved much serenity and acceptance of the world created by God. I find this a very good poem.

A PRAYER THAT WILL BE ANSWERED

Lord let me suffer much
and then die

Let me walk through silence
and leave nothing behind not even fear

Make the world continue
let the ocean kiss the sand just as before

Let the grass stay green
so that the frogs can hide in it

so that someone can bury his face in it
and sob out his love

Make the day rise brightly
as if there were no more pain

And let my poem stand clear as a windowpane
bumped by a bumblebee's head

Translated from the Polish by Stanislaw Barańczak and Clare Cavanagh

History

This chapter is in reality an anti-chapter. For poets of the twentieth century, history has been all-pervading, and much as they would like to turn to the eternal subjects of love and death, they have been forced to be aware of wars, revolutions, and the changes of political systems. Poets have been internally divided, knowing that they should serve art, but at the same time feeling a moral compulsion to be politically committed. The number of good and bad poems on the events of the twentieth century runs into many volumes. Yet still we lack the criteria to distinguish what, in all that number, is durable as the art of the word and what has its place as a document. But let us leave an assessment of the relations between poetry and history to our successors of the twenty-first century.

My reticence in filling this chapter with poems has a very personal explanation. Throughout some periods of my life, I have been a committed poet, active both as an author of verse and as an editor of publications directed against mass crimes. Thinking of those times, I rejoice in being able to make an anthology such as this one, and it may be a source of optimism that in this cruel century such an anthology could be made. And that is why I decided to make this chapter short, limiting it to poems in which I notice a high degree of distillation. By distillation I mean that only the most essential elements are left. In this respect, poetry of the countries most severely tried by the calamities of the twentieth century seems to be privileged, because their poets have given shape to those experiences in a most concise way. In this chapter, the poems I have selected are intended just as examples of poets' struggle in transmuting too crude and too cruel a reality into words through an artistic distance.

LEOPOLD STAFF
1878—1957

This poem was written immediately after World War II, in Poland, among the ruins, of which those in the figurative sense were even more oppressive than the physical ones. There was literally nothing. How could a poet react to that situation? What was left was to do what a child does, who when trying to draw a house often starts with the smoke from the chimney, then draws a chimney, and then the rest. So this is a poem of naked faith.

FOUNDATIONS

I built on the sand
And it tumbled down,
I built on a rock
And it tumbled down.
Now when I build, I shall begin
With the smoke from the chimney.

Translated from the Polish by Czeslaw Milosz

ANNA SWIR
1909—1984

Fire consumed the city of Warsaw. First, the part where the Germans had made the ghetto, and then the rest of the city. A lonely woman running through streets that are on fire is enough as a metaphor of a "limit situation."

I'M AFRAID OF FIRE

Why am I so afraid
running along this street
that's on fire.

After all there's no one here
only the fire roaring up to the sky
and that rumble wasn't a bomb
but just three floors collapsing.

Set free, the naked flames dance,
wave their arms
through the gaps of the windows,
it's a sin to peep at
naked flames
a sin to eavesdrop on
free fire's speech.

I am fleeing from that speech,
which resounded here on earth
before the speech of man.

Translated from the Polish by Magnus J. Krynski and Robert A. Maguire

ALEKSANDER WAT
1900—1967

The scene is a river somewhere in Soviet Asia. The helmsman is obviously a Muslim. The narrator is a poet deported by the Soviet authorities to Asia. All this setup is perhaps useful in seeing how such basic data are transformed into a parable on history as a dangerous and ominous force.

FROM PERSIAN PARABLES

By great, swift waters
on a stony bank
a human skull lay shouting:
Allah la ilah.

And in that shout such horror
and such supplication
so great was its despair
that I asked the helmsman:

What is there left to cry for? Why is it still afraid?
What divine judgment could strike it again?

Suddenly a rising wave
took hold of the skull
and tossing it about
smashed it against the bank.

Nothing is ever over
—the helmsman's voice was hollow—
and there is no bottom to evil.

Translated from the Polish by Czeslaw Milosz and Leonard Nathan

JULIA HARTWIG
1921—

Expectation of an imminent calamity. Many people have lived through such a moment, but they haven't left poems about it. Yet those moments are an integral part of history, of many cities and countries.

ABOVE US

Boys kicking a ball on a vast square beneath an obelisk
and the apocalyptic sky at sunset to the rear
Why the sudden menace in this view
as if someone wished to turn it all to red dust
The sun already knows And the sky knows it too
And the water in the river knows
Music bursts from the loudspeakers like wild laughter
Only a star high above us
stands lost in thought with a finger to its lips

Translated from the Polish by Stanisław Barańczak and Clare Cavanagh

SHU TING
1952—

This is a very ambiguous poem about something known to many people in this century, an ideological commitment to a cause, to a party, to a movement. One has had to cope not only with the inertia of the world but also with one's own doubt. Is the voice in this poem speaking for moving forward in spite of one's doubt, or, on the contrary, expressing the validity of doubt? We are not completely sure, either way.

PERHAPS . . .
for the loneliness of an author

Perhaps these thoughts of ours
            will never find an audience
Perhaps the mistaken road
            will end in a mistake
Perhaps the lamps we light one at a time
            will be blown out, one at a time
Perhaps the candles of our lives will gutter out
            without lighting a fire to warm us.

Perhaps when all the tears have been shed
            the earth will be more fertile
Perhaps when we sing praises to the sun
            the sun will praise us in return
Perhaps these heavy burdens
            will strengthen our philosophy
Perhaps when we weep for those in misery
            we must be silent about miseries of our own

Perhaps
Because of our irresistible sense of mission
We have no choice

Translated from the Chinese by Carolyn Kizer

RYSZARD KRYNICKI

1943–

The history of the twentieth century has been largely a history of mass crimes. Yet it has also witnessed the heroism of idealistically motivated men and women who were ready to offer their lives for the causes they believed sacred. This poem compares that faith in ideas to the urge of a moth to fly toward a candle, toward its destruction. By an ironic twist, in reality the poet praises the constant striving of people toward a dangerous goal.

I CAN'T HELP YOU

Poor moth, I can't help you,
I can only turn out the light.

Translated from the Polish by Stanislaw Barańczak and Clare Cavanagh

ZBIGNIEW HERBERT
1924—

The Castle of Elsinore has epitomized a place where an entanglement of will and fate is violently resolved and history is seen as tragedy. In modern interpretation the stress is laid upon the political aspect of Hamlet's situation, as a man surrounded by spies and pretending madness for self-protection. But Hamlet loses his game and everybody loses. Instead of heroic clashes of will, a provisional, patched-up status quo rules. The poem doesn't pronounce a clear judgment.

ELEGY OF FORTINBRAS

for C.M.

Now that we're alone we can talk prince man to man
though you lie on the stairs and see no more than a dead ant
nothing but black sun with broken rays
I could never think of your hands without smiling
and now that they lie on the stone like fallen nests
they are as defenceless as before. The end is exactly this
The hands lie apart The sword lies apart The head apart
and the knight's feet in soft slippers

You will have a soldier's funeral without having been a soldier
the only ritual I am acquainted with a little
There will be no candles no singing only cannon-fuses and
      bursts
crepe dragged on the pavement helmets boots artillery horses
       drums drums I know nothing exquisite
those will be my manoeuvres before I start to rule
one has to take the city by the neck and shake it a bit

Anyhow you had to perish Hamlet you were not for life
you believed in crystal notions not in human clay
always twitching as if asleep you hunted chimeras
wolfishly you crunched the air only to vomit
you know no human thing you did not know even how to
      breathe

Now you have peace Hamlet you accomplished what you
      had to
and you have peace The rest is not silence but belongs to me
you chose the easier part an elegant thrust
but what is heroic death compared with eternal watching
with a cold apple in one's hand on a narrow chair
with a view of the anthill and the clock's dial

Adieu prince I have tasks a sewer project
and a decree on prostitutes and beggars
I must also elaborate a better system of prisons
since as you justly said Denmark is a prison
I go to my affairs This night is born
a star named Hamlet We shall never meet
what I shall leave will not be worth a tragedy

It is not for us to greet each other or bid farewell we live on
      archipelagos
and that water these words what can they do what can they
      do prince

Translated by Czeslaw Milosz and Peter Dale Scott

MOUSHEGH ISHKHAN

1913 —

Armenians were the first to fall victim to genocide in the twentieth century.
Persecuted and dispersed, they have learned to live in exile in several countries and
on various continents. Since exile became the destiny of so many people in our
times, a poem on language is appropriate here. It extols an attachment to one's
mother tongue and a union through the language of all those who speak it.

THE ARMENIAN LANGUAGE
IS THE HOME OF THE ARMENIAN

The Armenian language is the home
and haven where the wanderer can own
roof and wall and nourishment.
He can enter to find love and pride,
locking the hyena and the storm outside.
For centuries its architects have toiled
to give its ceilings height.
How many peasants working
day and night have kept
its cupboards full, lamps lit, ovens hot.
Always rejuvenated, always old, it lasts
century to century on the path
where every Armenian can find it when he's lost
in the wilderness of his future, or his past.

Translated by Diana der Hovanessian

NAOMI LAZARD
1936—

Escapes over borders at the risk of one's life. Escapes on boats through dangerous seas. Long lines before consulates of happier countries. A dream of leaving behind oppression and misery. All this is a part of modern history, and for that reason this bitter poem acquires universal significance.

ORDINANCE ON ARRIVAL

Welcome to you
who have managed to get here.
It's been a terrible trip;
you should be happy you have survived it.
Statistics prove that not many do.
You would like a bath, a hot meal,
a good night's sleep. Some of you
need medical attention.
None of this is available.
These things have always been
in short supply; now
they are impossible to obtain.

        This is not
a temporary situation;
it is permanent.
Our condolences on your disappointment.
It is not our responsibility
everything you have heard about this place
is false. It is not our fault
you have been deceived,
ruined your health getting here.
For reasons beyond our control
there is no vehicle out.

CONSTANTINE CAVAFY
1863—1933

This poem has often been quoted, because it fits well the division of Europe, after
World War II, by the Cold War. Nobody seems to have paid attention to the date
of its writing, 1898. Cavafy, though he explored in his poems all the aspects of his
Hellenistic world, including the Greek-speaking Byzantine empire, understood the
word "barbarian" in its original Greek meaning, as applied to all those who are
outside and have, instead of human speech, incoherent gibberish. His intuition
allowed him to capture a centuries-old opposition between the inside and the outside
of civilization.

WAITING FOR THE BARBARIANS

What are we waiting for, assembled in the forum?

　　The barbarians are due here today.

Why isn't anything going on in the senate?
Why are the senators sitting there without legislating?

　　Because the barbarians are coming today.
　　What's the point of senators making laws now?
　　Once the barbarians are here, they'll do the legislating.

Why did our emperor get up so early,
and why is he sitting enthroned at the city's main gate,
in state, wearing the crown?

　　Because the barbarians are coming today
　　and the emperor's waiting to receive their leader.
　　He's even got a scroll to give him,
　　loaded with titles, with imposing names.

Why have our two consuls and praetors come out today
wearing their embroidered, their scarlet togas?
Why have they put on bracelets with so many amethysts,

rings sparkling with magnificent emeralds?
Why are they carrying elegant canes
beautifully worked in silver and gold?

    Because the barbarians are coming today
    and things like that dazzle the barbarians

Why don't our distinguished orators turn up as usual
to make their speeches, say what they have to say?

    Because the barbarians are coming today
    and they're bored by rhetoric and public speaking.

Why this sudden bewilderment, this confusion?
(How serious people's faces have become.)
Why are the streets and squares emptying so rapidly,
everyone going home lost in thought?

    Because night has fallen and the barbarians haven't come.
    And some of our men just in from the border say
    there are no barbarians any longer.

Now what's going to happen to us without barbarians?
Those people were a kind of solution.

Translated from the Greek by Edmund Keeley and Philip Sherrard

PERMISSIONS

Every effort has been made to obtain permission from the appropriate parties to include these works, but if any errors have been made we will be happy to correct them. We gratefully acknowledge the following permissions:

JUDAH AL-HARIZI. "The Lightning," "The Lute," and "The Sun," tr. T. Carmi, from *The Penguin Book of Hebrew Verse*, T. Carmi, ed. © 1981 by T. Carmi. Reprinted by permission of Penguin Books Ltd., UK.

JAMES APPLEWHITE. "Prayer for My Son" from *River Writing*. © 1988 by Princeton University Press. Reprinted by permission of Princeton University Press.

ALOYSIUS BERTRAND. "The Mason," tr. E. D. Hartley.

MIRON BIALOSZEWSKI. "A Ballad of Going Down to the Store" from *Postwar Polish Poetry*, Czeslaw Milosz, ed. Reprinted by permission of Bantam Doubleday Dell Publishing Group.

ELIZABETH BISHOP. "Brazil, January 1, 1502" from *The Complete Poems 1929–1979*. © 1983 by Alice Helen Methfessel. Reprinted by permission of Farrar, Straus & Giroux, Inc.

JOSEPH BRODSKY. "In the Lake District" and "Odysseus to Telemachus" from *A Part of Speech*. © 1980 by Farrar, Straus & Giroux, Inc. Reprinted by permission of Farrar, Straus & Giroux, Inc. and Oxford University Press, UK.

RAYMOND CARVER. "The Window" and "The Cobweb" from *Ultramarine*. © 1986 by Tess Gallagher. Reprinted by permission of Tess Gallagher. "Wine" from *A New Path to the Waterfall*. © 1989 by The Estate of Raymond Carver. Used by permission of Grove / Atlantic, Inc.

CONSTANTINE CAVAFY. "Waiting for the Barbarians," tr. Edmund Keeley, from *C. P. Cavafy: Collected Poems*. © 1975 by Edmund Keeley and Philip Sherrard. Reprinted by permission of Princeton University Press and Chatto & Windus. "Supplication" from *The Complete Poems of Cavafy*. © 1961 and renewed 1989 by Rae Dalven. Reprinted by permission of Harcourt Brace & Company.

BLAISE CENDRARS. "Aleutian Islands," "Fish Cove," "Frisco-City," "Harvest," and "South," tr. Monique Chefdor, from *Complete Postcards from the Americas: Poems of Road and Sea*. Monique Chefdor, tr. and ed. © 1976 by the Regents of the University of California. Reprinted by permission.

CHANG CHI. "Coming Late at Night to a Fisherman's Hut," tr. J. P. Seaton, from *Chinese Poetic Writing*. © by J. P. Seaton. Reprinted by permission of J. P. Seaton.

CHANG YANG-HAO. "Recalling the Past at T'ung Pass," trs. Gary Gach and C. H. Knock. Reprinted by permission of Gary Gach and C. H. Knock.

ALLEN GINSBERG. "A Strange New Cottage in Berkeley" from *Collected Poems 1947–1980*. © 1955 by Allen Ginsberg. Copyright renewed. Reprinted by permission of HarperCollins Publishers, Inc. and Penguin UK Ltd.

LINDA GREGG. "Adult" from *Alma*. © 1985 by Linda Gregg. Reprinted by permission of Random House, Inc. "A Dark Thing Inside the Day" and "Night Music" from *The Sacraments of Desire*. © 1991 by Linda Gregg. Reprinted with the permission of Graywolf Press, Saint Paul, MN.

EAMON GRENNAN. "Woman at a Lit Window" from *As If It Matters*. © 1991 by Eamon Grennan. Reprinted with the permission of Graywolf Press, Saint Paul, MN.

JORGE GUILLÉN. "Flight," tr. A. L. Geist, from *Guillen on Guillen: The Poetry and the Poet*, Jorge Guillen and Reginald Gibbons, eds. © 1979 by Princeton University Press. Reprinted by permission of Princeton University Press.

JOHN HAINES. "The Train Stops at Healy Fork" and "On the Mountain" from *News from the Glacier*. © 1982 by John Haines, Weslyan University Press. Reprinted by permission of University Press of New England.

JULIA HARTWIG. "Above Us," tr. Stanislaw Baranczak and Clare Cavanagh, from *Polish Poetry of the Last Two Decades of Communist Rule*. © 1991 by Northwestern University Press. Reprinted by permission of Northwestern University Press.

ROBERT HASS. "The Image" from *Praise*. © 1974–1979 by Robert Hass. First published by The Ecco Press in 1979. Reprinted by permission. "Late Spring" from *Human Wishes*. © 1989 by Robert Hass. First published by The Ecco Press in 1989. Reprinted by permission.

SEAMUS HEANEY. Excerpt from "Clearances" from *The Haw Lantern*. © 1987 by Seamus Heaney. Reprinted by permission of Farrar, Straus & Giroux, Inc. and Faber & Faber Ltd.

ZBIGNIEW HERBERT. "Elegy of Fortinbras" from *Postwar Polish Poetry*, Czeslaw Milosz, ed. Reprinted by permission of Bantam Doubleday Dell Publishing Group.

JANE HIRSHFIELD. "A Story" from *Of Gravity and Angels*. © 1988 by Jane Hirshfield, Weslyan University Press. Reprinted by permission of University Press of New England.

MOUSHEGH ISHKHAN. "The Armenian Language Is the Home of the Armenian," tr. Diana der Hovanessian. Reprinted by permission of Diana der Hovanessian.

ISSA. Haiku, trs. Lucien Stryk and Takashi Ikemoto, from *The Penguin Book of Zen Poetry*. Reprinted with the permission of Northern Illinois University Foundation.

ROLF JACOBSEN. "Cobalt," "Express Train," "Rubber," and "The Catacombs in San Callisto," tr. R. Greenwald, from *The Silence Afterwards: Selected Poems of Rolf Jacobsen*. © 1985 by Princeton University Press. Reprinted by permission of Princeton University Press.

ROBINSON JEFFERS. "Boats in Fog," "Carmel Point," "Cremation," and "Evening Ebb" from *Rock and Hawk*. © 1929 and renewed 1957 by Robinson Jeffers. Reprinted by permission of Random House, Inc.

ANNA KAMIEŃSKA. "A Prayer That Will Be Answered," tr. Stanislaw Baranczak and Clare Cavanagh, from *Polish Poetry of the Last Two Decades of Communist Rule*. © 1991

MUSO SOSEKI. "Magnificent Peak" and "Old Man at Leisure," tr. W. S. Merwin and Soiku Shigematsu, from *Sun at Midnight* by Muso Soseki. Reprinted by permission of W. S. Merwin and Soiku Shigematsu.

SOUTHERN BUSHMEN. "The Day We Die," tr. Arthur Markowitz.

LEOPOLD STAFF. "Foundations" from *Postwar Polish Poetry*, Czeslaw Milosz, ed. Reprinted by permission of Bantam Doubleday Dell Publishing Group.

WILLIAM STAFFORD. "Vacation" from *Stories That Could Be True.* © 1977 by William Stafford. Reprinted by permission of the Estate of William Stafford.

WALLACE STEVENS. "Study of Two Pears" from *Collected Poems.* © 1942 by Wallace Stevens and renewed 1970 by Holly Stevens. Reprinted by permission of Random House, Inc. and Faber & Faber Ltd.

SU MAN SHU. "Exile in Japan," tr. Kenneth Rexroth, from *Flower Wreath Hill.* © 1979 by Kenneth Rexroth. Reprinted by permission of New Directions Publishing Corp.

SU TUNG P'O. "On a painting by Wang the Clerk," tr. Kenneth Rexroth, from *Flower Wreath Hill.* © 1979 by Kenneth Rexroth. Reprinted by permission of New Directions Publishing Corp.

MAY SWENSON. "Question" from *The Complete Poems to Solve.* © 1993 by The Literary Estate of May Swenson. Reprinted with permission of Simon & Schuster Books for Young Readers, an imprint of Simon & Schuster Children's Publishing Division.

ANNA SWIR. "The Greatest Love," "I Starve My Belly for a Sublime Purpose," "I Talk to My Body," "I Wash the Shirt," "Poetry Reading," "The Same Inside," "The Sea and the Man," "She Does Not Remember," "The Second Madigral," and "Troubles with the Soul at Morning Calisthentics," trs. Czeslaw Milosz and Leonard Nathan, from *Talking to My Body.* © 1996 by Anna Swir. "I'm Afraid of Fire" tr. Czeslaw Milosz. Reprinted by permission of Copper Canyon Press, P.O. Box 271, Port Townsend, WA 98368.

WISLAWA SZYMBORSKA. "In Praise of Self-Deprecation," "Four in the Morning," "Seen from Above," and "In Praise of My Sister," tr. Magnus J. Krynski and Robert A. Macguire, from *Sounds, Feelings, Thoughts: Seventy Poems.* © 1981 by Princeton University Press. Reprinted by permission of Princeton University Press. "View with a Grain of Sand," tr. Stanislaw Baranczak and Clare Cavanagh, from *Polish Poetry of the Last Two Decades of Communist Rule.* © 1991 by Northwestern University Press. Reprinted by permission of Northwestern University Press.

JAMES TATE. "Teaching the Ape to Write Poems" from *Absences: New Poems.* © 1970, 1971, 1972 by James Tate. By permission of Little, Brown and Company.

TOMAS TRANSTRÖMER. "Outskirts" and "Tracks" from *Selected Poems 1954–1986.* © 1985 by John F. Deane and Tomas Tranströmer; © 1975 by Robert Bly and Tomas Tranströmer. First published by The Ecco Press in 1987. Reprinted by permission. "Syros," trs. May Swenson and Leif Sjöberg. © 1972. Reprinted by permission of the University of Pittsburgh Press.

TU FU. "Travelling Northward," "Sunset," "Winter Dawn," "South Wind," "Clear After Rain," "To Pi Ssu Yao," and "Snow Storm," tr. Kenneth Rexroth, from *Collected Shorter Poems* by Kenneth Rexroth. © 1956, 1944, 1963 by Kenneth Rexroth. Reprinted by permission of New Directions Publishing Corp. "Coming Home Late

INDEX OF AUTHORS

INDEX OF TITLES OR FIRST LINES